UNDICI
Eleven Ways That Vermont Is Going Down The Johnny Flusher

DOMINIC M. MARTIN

UNDICI: ELEVEN WAYS THAT VERMONT IS GOING DOWN THE JOHNNY FLUSHER

iUniverse books may be ordered through booksellers or by contacting:

iUniverse
1663 Liberty Drive
Bloomington, IN 47403
www.iuniverse.com
844-349-9409

ISBN: 978-1-4502-0491-0 (sc)
ISBN: 978-1-4502-0492-7 (e)

Print information available on the last page.

iUniverse rev. date: 09/02/2025

CONTENTS

PREFACE

Because my brother went there eight years earlier and since I am, like so many others, habit's son, I attended Gonzaga University in Spokane, Washington. I was only 17 when I first started and had what might be generously called an "uncertain complexion." But my youth and pimples did not stop me from learning from those unstern Jesuits; they taught us logic, ethics, the dangers of moral relativism, and how to separate mores from morals, cant and drivel from proper thought. Those two years, combined with four earlier at an Augustinian High School (Villanova) were solid preparation for my next turn in the road: the University of California at Santa Cruz.

At that time it was the archetypal hippie school. Sometimes it seemed that everyone had long hair, hated the Establishment, had sex with people like changing a shirt and used drugs purchased from whomever was nearby. Most, if not all, of the professors were very liberal, or else, borderline socialists. In those now long distant days, though the lesbian agenda was only slowly simmering, most of the coeds (may I call them that?) attempted to look like guys: flannel shirts, heavy hiking boots, and hairy everything. My love life was fumbling and paltry, mostly composed of incipient unfocused yearnings. Years there passed when I never saw a curved bronzed calf or the tantalizing beginnings of a soft breast. Perfume? Not a chance. In the classroom the students often asserted their disdain and irrationality to the non-delight of the teachers who, yet, protested little. Religion, especially the Catholic Church, was routinely mocked, as well as most rules, statutes and limitations, and today, I regret not defending my faith more vigorously.

One day a classmate of mine said to me that there was going to be a party somewhere and that there would be some 'good drugs." (These were my luxuriant, carefree days of youth when I would go to gatherings to eat more than anything else: I joked that I had a coat with plastic pockets to bring food home.) I quickly wondered: "What the hell are good drugs, besides penicillin if you have tuberculosis?" For those six years of Catholic education gave to me a quick skepticism that would be sorely needed if I were to stay afloat at UCSC, and not lose myself in that school's implied promotion of values and contrary to what I knew and thought. Now, that same skepticism allows me to look at the rampaging social experiment that is Vermont and, further, ask myself many questions about how it has changed from a farming state and where it probably headed.

Back in high school at Villanova, we had a coach named Elmo Ferrari. He did everything: he taught history, Spanish and typing, coached all three sports and was the Athletic Director. He was ex-Marine, a bachelor and a diabetic. Though short, he was solid and would not back down from any lippy senior, however muscled or tall. He used to say to us on Friday afternoon: "If any of you guys this weekend try anything you shouldn't with girls, if you drink, if you use drugs, if you steal something, if you race cars, if you disrespect your mothers or fathers, on Monday morning I will know by the guilty look on your faces and I will kick your ass. You will wish that you had behaved yourself. Now, get out of here." Some guys thought he was extreme, but I loved him. I broke my right arm two times playing mediocre basketball for him. He taught me a lot about discipline and having a work ethic: he said that all good things had to be earned. This idea would become important when we moved to Vermont where so many things are given away for free.

Ferrari saved some of the guys in school, some of those types that thought it was a cracker-jack idea to use LSD or steal some stereos. Also, he taught us how to cuss properly: probably because of his years in the Marines, he was a professional cusser.

Ferrari never noticed me because when I was a freshman, I was only 5-feet tall and weighed 100 pounds. I wager that he was looking for someone with little more beef or heft, but that is just a guess. We all feared Ferrari because he was a profane as hell and, especially, because he had been to war and anyone could tell how that had changed him and made him harder: there floated about his person an aura that said that the world is mean and sad and unrelenting and that, nonetheless, I must remain strong. Whenever he threatened us, we knew that he would never do anything to hurt us and that he was only trying to help a bunch of lazy piss ants. Now, of course, that use of an unmitigated fear, a tool to encourage responsibility, is gone and we are all the worse off for that loss.

Of course, it starts earlier with my parents. My mom was the kind and nurturing sort and my dad, the stern, drill sergeant variety. Actually, having been in the Navy during World War II as a navigator, he was more the yelling boatswain. They were the typical good cop/ bad cop parents. When I did something wrong my mom would gently chastize me and say: "You don't want your father to have to speak to you about this, do you?" No, I did not. He was tall and strong and impressibly built, like William Holden or Ward Bond. He had a booming voice that would scare the monkeys out of the trees.

They were both pretty conservative, my dad especially. In the early 60s he was darn near obsessed with Communists' expansion plans around the world. He wanted Castro out of Cuba yesterday. When the Bay of Pigs happened in April of 1961 he cursed John Kennedy for a couple of hours straight. When my mom told him to calm down or else he would have a heart attack (she knew since she was a nurse) he yelled, "Cram it, Florence. Don't you realize what is happening right before our eyes?" When he said, "before our eyes" he would lean forward from the waist and his eyebrows would go up high and his neck would twist like a helix. It was a little spooky.

One Friday night, I had a buddy for a sleep-over. At the dinner table and after having drunk a few glasses of red wine, my dad was really getting his engine going: he was talking about Castro's plans in Africa; he was saying that he communists wanted to take over the world. He didn't stop talking; little bits of white spittle formed at the edge of his mouth. My mom tried to change the conversation, but no dice. Suddenly, with almost a leering glance at me, he asked my buddy, "So, what do you think about Angola?" My friend's face went blank. He blushed. His eyes darted back and forth. And, then he said, "It's a heck of a motorcycle. But, sometime the clutch is hard to pull in." My dad looked at me and smiled, and then he looked at my buddy and said, "You're absolutely right, young man, and sometimes the carburetor is easy to flood." Then he had another big glass of wine and gazed at my mom with a silly, half-drunk smile.

When I was that pimply, seventeen year old going away to college, he bought for me a subscription to *National Review*. He said I would need it "to keep my brain from going to mush or rancid oatmeal."

He was right. I still subscribe to it today. It provides a useful counterpoint to the constant liberal bias in the media today. Where is the tried and true objectivity of, say, the old news team of Huntley and Brinkley? Today much of the media tells you what to think rather than presenting facts (not the propaganda) and then letting you decide on your own.

So, these short pieces that follow, charting as they do the slide of Vermont towards extremism, alternative lifestyles, progressiveness, socialism or whatever other word you might choose that reflects the Robin Hood or liberal social engineering mentality, these brief pieces, their tone and tack, they reflect the traditional education and religious upbringing that

I was very lucky to have received. My parents, my priests and teachers, my coach, Elmo Ferrari, all of them would be appalled at what is going on in Vermont today. Maybe my dad, the crusty South Pacific navigator, actually wrote these stories and not I. Why, if I listen hard enough I can truly hear my dad whisper in my ear, "That place is going down the tubes and here's how!"

CHAPTER ONE:
An Expensive Lawn mower

We had just moved there, that is, to Vermont, the lovely and verdant Green Mountain State full of misty variegated hills and trickling creeks, and we all had more to do than could even possibly be accomplished. Who has the light bulbs, where is the vacuum cleaner, what's for dinner? Our goods had arrived in a battered 40 foot container and endless trips were required, up stairs, down hallways, across thresholds. Some rooms became quickly overcrowded, instantly going from bedroom to warehouse. I made the small admonition, "Let us not move anything twice. Take it only once to where it finally belongs," a warning which was understandably ignored. Days went by shuffling, lugging, shifting boxes, furniture, clothes. Would here be no end? Our goods became a mountain of salt that one tries to move by means of the smallest spoon. I know that each of us, my wife, and our three children, lost a few pounds so great was our exertion and so small our ingestion. Some complained of itchy, frozen backs. I came down with plantar fascitis, a painful inflammation of the sole's fascia. I hobbled about the messy and chaotic house like an old man, half-drunken, might look for his pipe or glasses. And then one day, so hobbling, I went to a window to the backyard and, there leaning for support, saw the fields around us more than a foot high with gras. Alas! Another job to do! Who can do it? Not I!

As it happened, we lived close to a nursery, and, figuring that they would own a lawn tractor and have someone to run it, I asked them for help. They said yes, and a couple days later, Jeremy showed up. He was a short fellow, and friendly enough. I heard the rumbling of the tractor just behind him. It was 10AM and, as I went back to shuffling my mountain of salt with my teaspoon, he began to mow.

As he worked I could hear the spitfire rumblings of the machine and, occasionally, a loud bang or clank when he hit a large rock or tree stump. Soon, in exactly three hours time, he appeared again at the backdoor and said he was finished. I took a quick peak and saw that he had done a good job. So I asked him how much we owed him and he said quickly: "120."

I said to myself, that is way too low: 40 cents an hour is not enough! Then, a stirring took place in my small Irish pea-brain: Jeremy expects me to pay him, a sophomore in high school, 40 **dollars** an hour. He wants $120 for the three hour job! Flustered, confused, but not yet angry, I wrote him out the check. Unhappy with a check, he said, while leaving, that he would have preferred to have received cash. Not wishing to be stung twice, we never hired him again.

The point of this short vignette is to ask ourselves the question: "How is it that his sixteen year old might plausibly think that he is worth $40 per hour?" The answer is that, the work ethic shifted profoundly.

In my youth, everyone had a summer job; it was simply expected! Most were full time and paid poorly. Some were dangerous. Many involved working with illegal Mexicans, tending to citrus trees, spraying, planting, pruning. If one had a strict father, like I did, someone who had reached physical maturity just as the Great Depression arrived at its crushing nadir, then one inherited (or had thrust upon!) a work ethic, just like a son gets from his father, thinning hair or keen eyesight. No one <u>did</u> <u>not</u> work. All of my friends worked at least 40 hours a week. Some of their parents expected that the money earned, or most of it, would be placed in the family's kitty, to be used to buy groceries or gasoline. Rarely was there the squeak of protest; most teenagers then understood that one had to contribute to the family's welfare. Weekends, only, were for fun, and chores. My father would give me a list of things to do on a Saturday morning and complain when I did not finish all the items on the list, saying that I could have got them all done if I had been more organized. Scoldings for a less than perfect effort were common and expected.

How times have changed! Laws that control adolescent labor have been strongly applied and enforced but in truth, these laws have engendered a generation of perpetual kids, a sissy nation, (Indeed, read John Strausbaugh's book : *Sissy Nation*. Virgin Books, 2007.) But, more than that, parents no longer expect their teenagers to work, or to help out with the family's expenses. Gone is the sensible idea that amusement can take place only after the work is done, the chores are finished, or that job painting the garage is completed. Absent is the prudent idea that fun is only fun when it is balanced by work. So, today, most teenagers are free all summer, free to socialize, free to roam, free to pursue whatever fleeting interests or desires that they might conjure. Amusement, not work, has become paramount. Labor, now, is seen by youth as something that is boring and old-fashioned, something for other people to do. The idea that a vacation can only be fulfilling because, before it, the work was done has been lost. And that notion has been supplanted, because of a parent's lassitude or a teenagers' eagerness for fun, with the bald thought that I am free to have fun anytime and any way that I can get it.

Of course, the repercussions of all of this are vast. Today's youth, once they are parents, are unlikely to engender a work ethic in their children, since they have never seen one. Secondly, so much work is farmed out, mostly to illegal Mexican workers who ably perform the work most of today's teenagers deride. Third, in a subtle way, since most teenagers lack this work ethic, the fabric of society – that we can all work together , has been rent. Finally, we are breeding children full of ever-expanding expectations, those without governance or limit. Does all of this not mean that these disinclined-to-work teenagers, once adult, will not be able to work since that habit will never have been acquired? But, more than anything else, a nation that cannot pick its own fruits and vegetables and whose people do not grasp the intrinsic value to all work, however menial or common, that country is in serious trouble.

CHAPTER TWO:
Fence | Tractor | Pond

One of the many attributes to our beautiful, small ranch was the existence of a tiny pond, certainly less than an acre, located "out back" on the edge of our box alder woods. With some probing by stick I could determine that it was, in spots at least, fairly deep, over five feet. When we moved to Vermont from leafy Somerset, England, our" littlest small fry," was only one and a half years old and just starting to walk. So, with scant thought and little hesitation, I judged that a small fence was needed to encircle the pond, to prevent her drowning, only on those lands which were ours, and, as quickly as I could, I erected said fence, and then slept the better for having done so.

The next day I received a phone call from a neighbor. Not irate but questioning, he asked why I had put up such an ugly fence. I told him that such an ugly fence was needed to prevent our daughter, just starting to walk, from a possible drowning.

He, I felt, was not entirely satisfied with the reasoning, yet rang off.

Not long afterward, approaching our first Spring in Vermont when all proper husbandmen wish to work up the soil, rid it of pernicious winter weeds and plant, I saw our neighbor driving a small lawn tractor plus a cart or open wagon across our fields. By the glazed grass and a deepening rut I adjudged that he had made many trips to a nearly nursery to purchase bulk compost which, I guessed, he intended to use later to ameliorate his garden's soil. He had not asked beforehand whether we would allow him to make these many trips across our land.

Not wanting a fight but clearly irked, I asked our neighbor what he was doing. He said that he was getting some composted soil for his garden. I asked him why he did not take the county road to procure the soil. He said that he was trying to save gas. I told him that he needed permission and that, because of the ever-deepening ruts and the glazed grass, such permission would not be granted. He said that he had not asked for permission in advance because in many prior years he had purchased the soil in the same exact manner and that he did not think we would mind. He did not in the least apologize and thus commenced our growing stalemate.

About this same time, as we were settling in, during which time our children incrementally lost their British accents, we noticed that people drove down our street sometimes very quickly, often over 60 mph, though the posted speed limit was 35 mph. Accordingly, we contacted a nearby fence company and had them install a 4-foot, red cedar fence, one not solid but open and lapped, at the road's edge.

Not long afterwards, an angry woman entered our garage and yelled profanities at a couple of older workers that we had hired. She was so angry that she was largely unintelligible, but with concentration, the jist was this: that the fence was dangerous since it restricted her ability to view down the street for approaching cars, before pulling out onto the road.

I asked some of our neighbors what they thought, whether they agreed with the angry and profane woman, and one lady memorably said that whenever you drive in the country you have to be careful. I wanted to give her a peck on the cheek.

One day, as I recall, we spoke directly with the angry neighbors. They, the husband and wife, said that the fence was dangerous, that it restricted their line of sight, and that it was possibly within the town's 25-foot right of way. I said that the perception of dangerousness was highly subjective, and that I was unaware of any possible right-of-way infringement. I said that reasonable people can disagree or arrive at completely opposite opinions. No threats were issued and no voices raised, but once again commenced, tinged by a slightly rancorous odor, another stalemate.

Time passed. We forgot about the issue; was that wise? From our fence-hating neighbors, hand waves decreased. Eye contact went away. And one day we received a letter from the town saying that our cedar fence had to be moved backwards towards the house, around seven feet, as I remember.

We complied, unhappily. Is this the way small matters of dispute are to be settled? Is this the best and proper way for neighbors to behave towards one another? What does this dispute say about our society's declining ability to discuss, let alone, compromise? What do all three of these admittedly petty arguments declare about tolerance, or the lessening possibility of debate. Must there always be a law that is the causal factor?

Robert Frost wrote, "Good fences make good neighbors." He was writing about New England, back in the long gone day when everyone pretty much minded their own business, where you didn't put your nose underneath someone else's tent.

It was with that false assumption that we moved to Vermont. False, because Frost is speaking about the <u>old</u> New England. New England has changed. All of America has changed, in ways serpentine and incremental, subtle and undiagnosed.

Let us consider, for example, the small issues of land use mentioned here. Many Vermonters, and especially those recently arrived, believe that private property is a misnomer, that it should not exist, that all property should be public. Many believe that trespassing laws should not be enforced. Many think that private property is not really private, or that ownership is underneath it all in some mysterious way, shared. Communal rights become paramount and personal rights correspondingly diminish. Therefore, trespassing can be excused, if not encouraged.

There is another, concluding side to this debate. Now, and with the passage of time, I believe that all three of these silly arguments were engendered by the facts that we were, and are, a conservative Catholic family. If we had been part of the progressive movement these fights would not have started. Other, less severe ways would have been favored to solve the problems. As soon as some of our neighbors heard that we did not send our children to the local public school (where diversity is all!) but, rather, to a Catholic school, as soon as they saw back in 2004 our George Bush poster of support, as soon as they heard me rail about out-of-control property taxes, we were part of the problem and to be scorned. Thus, small fights started, fed by normal political disagreements. Because we were not part of their counter cultural club or team, a member of their nearly socialist program, differences grew to the point of heckling, harassment, argument, and what should have been a normal tolerant neighborhood instead became one steeped in rancor and discord.

How has all this happened? Why is tolerance so diminished? Why are neighborhood rifts, like these three, so common? The answer is this: starting around 1965 people began to move to those states or areas where, they assumed, people would accept and appreciate their shared views. (Read Bill Bishop and Robert G. Cushing. <u>The Big Sort: Why the Clustering of Like-Minded America is Tearing Us Apart</u>. Houghton Mifflin Company, 2008). Homosexuals moved to San Francisco, neo-Nazis migrated to Idaho, and near socialists traveled to Vermont. In 1960 Vermont voted for Nixon, but a few decades later the state could reasonably be described as a progressive's haven. When we first moved to Vermont, we did not fully understand just how extreme the state has became, how large the safety net is, and how detailed are its denizens' plans for ever greater diversity. When you think of all of this factors, it is no wonder that our welcome there was so muted.

All of this is sad and troubling. It means that friendship, in a state more intolerant everyday, is very hard to establish. Before a friendship may be established, 100% political agreement must be achieved. What ever happened to our ability to debate freely, actively, even harshly and, then, forget about it and have a beer or laugh? Friendship is lost or not even attempted. Bobby Jones said in a memoir, "Friends are a man's priceless treasure." Because of our growing intractability and our disinclination to openly debate and happily disagree, more and more, as a country and as a people, we are losing this treasure. What difference does it make if you and I disagree on euthanasia, stem-cell research or abortion: are we not all Americans? Have we not all been handed the greatest country on earth in which to live? Yet we diminish it daily by stubbornness and obstinacy. It is said that the more degrees a person has after his name, the less likely he is to discuss issues with someone who holds the opposite opinion. That sort of contrary intolerance, which now plagues Vermont and much of the country as a whole, needs to be first recognized and then stopped. Otherwise, there is this thing about stalemates: they never end.

CHAPTER THREE:
Ginesti and an Australian

Usually, when one moves to a new region, most of one's neighbors will express some curiosity: "Where have you come from? How long were you there? Why did you move here?" After all, we had a had an interesting story to tell: 25 years in the wine business, a British wife, three years in Somerset, England, considerable time in Italy, especially Trieste. Yet, once we moved to Vermont, few questions were asked of us. The point of this short piece in to answer this question: Is this normal, old-fashioned Yankee taciturnity, or perhaps rectitude; or, is there some other, perhaps more snotty factor at work?

Here it is crucial to note that only approximately 660,000 people live in Vermont, and that number includes two groups or what we call "camps": the old Vermonters and the new Vermonters. Old Vermonters are disinclined to bother others; also, they are frugal with money and they are hard working. They, generally speaking, want government to stay out of their lives and to therefore tax them only slightly. New Vermonters, recently arrived from all over the country but especially from urban areas of the Northeast, have much more money than the older camp, allowing them to purchase nicer homes. Many have independent trust funds from which they derive a steady income. As a group they are very well educated, most having secured college degrees. They are opinionated and extremely liberal, and are not shy about expressing those views. And finally, they make the assumption that all others agree with them on all issues.

Many new Vermonters use a cunning strategy when meeting a stranger: the new Vermonter liberal assumes that the stranger holds nothing but progressive opinions. They will say, for example, that "assisted death is a good idea," or "Isn't our president an ass?" without thinking whether this type of speech is courteous. And the result is off-putting: the stranger may feel, immediately, slightly belittled. On the other hand, the progressive, not recognizing his or her own rudeness, blithely continues on, unaware, perhaps looking for another stranger to insult. This is a not-so-subtle form of one-upmanship, a mean-spirited type of negotiation that ought to be curtailed.

This immigration of Vermonters to the Green Mountain State started in the mid-60s. I can recall how, back in the early 70s, at my extremely liberal California college, the word went out: "Vermont is the best place to which to migrate." Why? Someone said: "The dope is good. The rent is low. Food stamps are easy to get. And people there think like you," notwithstanding the fact that no one at my extremely liberal

California college ever asked me what I thought, or for that matter, cared.

Now, time has passed. By now, aging hippies have made it their home for decades. Their progressive views have tinctured the state on every level: land use policy (Act 250), civil unions, property tax, drug law enforcement, school funding (Act 60), child molestation, etc.... It is amazing to learn that at the state house in Montpelier, approximately 67% of the lawmakers are not native Vermonters. A huge social experiment has thus ensured, whereby the new Vermonters have been able to "engineer" an untraditional society in which their progressive social view may be tested. But more than anything else affecting neighborhoods, it is their personal insularity which is difficult to understand.

One day, at my young son's baseball game, I met a fellow father named Ginesti. I was intrigued with him and his name and, because I am keen on all things Italian, I asked him if he were. He said that he was Swiss, but acted disinterested, bored, insular. I told him that his name reminded me of ginestra, the mountain broom or gorse from which in the Dolomites that the most intoxicating distillates are made, and that many contadini there attribute long life to these strong, artisanal "bosco" brews. After that small speech, he said little. I mentioned that we ought to get together, since both our families had lived in Europe for awhile, our children were the same ages and we lived quite close to each other, in fact, in the same neighborhood. Ahem! It was at that point that I realized that I had awkwardly reached too far: he did not wish to be my friend. He did not desire our families to share time or jokes or food or wine together. I felt myself a fool, and he drifted off, waving a lame arm as goodbye, and the two of us never spoke again.

Another day not too long after that day, I was at the enormous soccer field, watching my son play soccer. Having little to do but being naturally curious, I struck up a conversation (my earlier shyness having disappeared about the same time that my stomach's paunce arrived) with an Australian fellow and father. He had been all over the world I discovered: Australia, Switzerland, England. For a time he had been educated in Dorset, England. "Really?, " I said, "that is where my in-laws reside. Did you go to the Sherborne School perhaps?"

"Yes," he said, "in fact, I did."

"Did you take Mathematics from a certain Professor _____?"

"Yes, in fact I did," he said.

My father-in-law 15 years earlier had taught him some level of Algebra, and here we were thousands of miles distant reminiscing about those old times. Or, should I say, I was, since he, like Ginestri, was distinctly not interested in our conversation. And soon, it stalled and he wandered off. At least that day it did not get to the embarrassing point where I said, making a fool of myself, 'let's get together."

It is difficult to make friends as a man grows older. (All appropriate apologies, Svevo.) One, perhaps, already <u>has</u> friends. There are the distracting pressures of work, the busyness of family. Some people view another as a possible friend only if that person might be of some use (Here, I nod to Seneca.), and since I would not be useful that friendship need not be pursued.

But, I believe that in Vermont and, no doubt, in many other places as well that there is something unique at play. Because of this insularity of the people moving in and of the New Vermonters already arrived, little curiosity about others exists, which, in turn, leads to fewer friendships. Gone are the days there when you know everyone on the block. Gone are the days when you cold trust other parents to discipline your children if they got out of line. Gone are the days when free and open debate, concluded without rancor, was something that you looked forward to. Now, in Vermont and especially during those long winter days when the sun, weak, barely rises in the sky, we are locked away, billeted in our homes, barracks, sequestered with our own rutted thoughts, independent yes, but less connected than ever before to society's fabric, the neighbor's pull or push. Society is less now, and technology has had a huge role to play here; but it is our insular attitudes that have made this growing separateness happen. Curiosity is mostly departed now, and I fear that the situation grows worse all the time. If the lost, gentle art of conversation cannot be resurrected, the situation I have described will only further deteriorate. Neighbors used to argue over the side fence, or, on a good day, kindly disagree. Today most are ensconced at a personal computer, blogging, speaking digitally to someone half way round the world. Human contact has thus lessened. But we should ask ourselves "Is this insularity preferable? Is this the type of world that is best? Some questions: and how did all this happen?

CHAPTER FOUR:
Public School versus Catholic School

Whenever I took my son to a Little League game (three beautiful fields surrounded by berry fields. I noticed that the top horizontal member of the outfield fence, in another nod to victimhood, was covered in a bright yellow plastic so that if one of the kids dove for a ball nearly out of the ballpark, he would not be impaled.), other parents would say to me, even though we had been there for two years, "you must be new."

"No," I said, "We send our three kids to the Catholic school in Burlington." Now, here, of course, the reaction would vary from derision to curiosity. But many, if not most, when I told them that we preferred Catholic education (and were prepared to pay for it), many would look at me like I had two heads, three ears, five eyes. So exalted is the status of public education in their eyes that many took it as a personal affront that we eschewed it.

When we left Vermont in 2007, it had achieved, by intent, one of the most expensive public school systems in the country, spending $10,000 a year for each elementary student, and 50% more than that for each high school student. Class sizes are usually very small, around 15-20. The best food, the finest athletic facilities, the most elaborate education back-up support and aides and all the rest are routinely employed. The teachers receive the most generous health care benefits around and when the insurance carrier raises the premium at a rate well above inflation, these added insurance costs are usually added to the budget, to be paid for by unsuspecting taxpayers. Opportunities to "pool buy" insurance, that is, to purchase insurance on a state-wide basis instead of by district or county, are neglected. Efforts to consolidate the hundreds of districts in the state, to save money and improve efficiencies, are fought. Capital improvements are carried out annually across the state, based on foolish expectations of enrollment. And, it is worthwhile to note, roughly 25% of Vermont high school students drop out, never graduating: whatever happened to the old-style Truant Officer, with a cap and a badge and a very stern look?

Because of the always escalating cost-of-living in Vermont, traceable to a burgeoning property tax rate used to pay for these public schools, many people can no longer afford to live there. The average family with two kids, a dog and a cat, is being forced out; many leave for the South where the expectation about what society ought to do for the individual is much less. It is estimated that the number of high school graduates in five years will have decreased by 50%. This should make the class size really small, and the cost of educating each student very large!

Back in the day, when the Browns had just left St. Louis and become the Orioles, when the Brockton Bomber was champ, and the Brooklyn Dodgers had just won their only World Championship, that is, back in 1956 (Eisenhower has suffered a heart attack but kept it pretty quiet. He ruled things from the Gettysburg Inn and wondered when he could get back to the golf course), I entered first grade. Speaking of class size, there were 83 of us, grabbing, spitting, pulling, pushing, some so nervous that they were ready to puke; the poor nun whose name, like much else, I cannot recall: she had too much to do!

That first morning a large red-faced Irish fireman came into the classroom to inspect "our safety." He said in a loud, accented voice, "Sister, half these kids have got to go!" Well, some of us, the more nervous amongst us, heard the verb "go" and understood that we had permission to tinkle there in the desk, to micturate, to urinate, to pee; and so, many of us, perhaps a dozen (but not I, not I!) of us went ahead and did so in front of the gasping nun and the Irish fireman who said, "Goodbye for now, Sister; I can see you have your hands full. God bless!"

About 15 years ago the teachers came up with this idea that kids cannot learn if the class size is above 25. Small class size became the mantra, the idea that was constantly pushed: if you love your child, you must believe this. One obvious consequence of this has been a huge increase in the number of teachers, teachers' aides and all manner of assistants. And, in the process, the budgets have increased at a pace well above inflation. This is now a crisis across the country. In Vermont in those 5 years that we lived there, it was routine to see annual school budget increases of 6 or 7 or 8 percent, that compared to an inflation rate of 2 or 3. But, because public education has been put on a pedestal by most, but especially by New Vermonters (those recently arrived with perhaps a slightly fatter wallet), these annual budget increases were normally approved by a wide margin.

State ordered mandates, often engendered by teachers' lobbying groups in the various state capitols across the country, compel under force of law, schools to do this or do that, usually at very high cost. Common sense and local control, or indeed, the prerogative of the principal, have been tossed aside, replaced by state-ordered mandates. Most of these mandates have been engineered by teachers themselves and it is rare to see among them much efficiency or usefulness to the children themselves. Teachers do not wish to stress the fundamental ironic fact that, despite all this extra spending, the student' test scores remain flat.

Catholic schools operate more modestly, spending in rough numbers, perhaps one third the amount that public education does. Their teachers are paid much less, the benefit and pension packages are paltry by comparison, and the facilities, especially the athletic ones, are not fancy. Yet, education does take place, and Catholic graduates usually do better on standardized tests, and, some would argue, later in life. But many New Vermonters do not believe in God. One of the things that they like about public education is that it essentially precludes any discussion of a Deity. Remember that this is the generation that back in the 70s declared: "GOD IS DEAD."

Even though our coins say "IN GOD WE TRUST," we cannot pray aloud in school. This is something that many of the aging hippies and baby boomers, think is a good thing since they believe that religion has only caused wars and engendered a useless and false guilt. And, of course, once God is dead, one is free to adopt any amoral code on a daily basis depending on what seems like a good idea at the time.

Eventually, as the budgets become even more bloated and as the number of school-age children continues to fall, perhaps there will be a small revolt. Maybe someone will say, "Shop around for a better insurance deal. Consolidate!" or "Restrict your budget to inflation and not a penny more!" With their always hungry appetite for more pay, greater pensions and more secure and larger pensions, the school teachers in many states, but especially Vermont, remind me of the autoworkers of the 70s: eventually they will harm the industry they serve. But when the state's main newspaper everyday seeks to sanctify public education, such a revolution will be difficult.

Ironic that word: "sanctify" means to make something sacred. Godliness, inviolate saintliness, words that ought to be applied to a church or a holy person. But since for many New Vermonters and perhaps some Old, public education has become a religion, perhaps it makes a certain sad sense.

In truth, of course, education is not a religion, and nor is yoga, cell phones, fast cars or marijuana. Thinking it so does not make it happen, just as declaring God dead does not kill him. How far we have gone off track! Many public schools in Vermont teach that having two mommies or two daddies is just fine. Indeed, some say that those family situations are preferable. Everywhere feminism has marginalized fatherhood and encouraged non-traditional families. Catholic schools teach the opposite: that gay marriage is contrary to God's plan and that homosexuality should not be encouraged.

Whither shall we turn? Will the diversity doctrine still be the standard? What kind of society will Vermont offer in twenty or thirty years once these deleterious factors have been in place for a further generation? Will vouchers become popular, allowing parents, read taxpayers, the chance to choose what sort of schooling their children will receive?

I do not think so. Vermont has turned a corner. The far-left, secular progressives have won too many battles. The diversity dictum cannot be touched. Public education, though it be but chalk and talk, Shakespeare and division, has become a religion, at least in the dim eyes of some, though it is not, though it is not. No one ever looks back to see what we spend on education in the 50s, 60s, or 70s and to find out how well those students did, despite modest spending. Is there not a point at which, as spending on public education increases, it is actually <u>counter</u>-productive? Excuse me for such heresy!

And, I do not care what you say; I still think that girls are pretty!

CHAPTER FIVE:
Block Party, and Then?

Every year on our street a block party was held, the location rotating from house to house based on some arcane formula. The guest hosts provided food and drink, party favors of some kind, and something sweet for the kids to eat and drink. One had to be very careful what food was offered because so many of the neighbors has very stringent, need I say, picky requests.

One day I started talking to one of our neighbors about coffee (I cannot recall how this started), and she asked me if I ground my beans. "Sometimes," I said. This disappointed her because it showed a lack of care, and little attention to detail. With her slight frown was I being criticized? Then she asked, "What kind of grinder do you use?" She explained that some actually prevent essential oils from being carried over to the brew. I tried not to smirk, but resolved not to serve coffee when we hosted the party: I would do it wrong!

That year my wife would host the party alone since I

would be out-of-town that day. I did not want to miss it, but life is full of those kinds of conflicts. I suggested to my wife, that she stock up lots of white wine and a local summer ale spiced with grains of paradise, a peppery African spice, which was thought to be an aphrodisiac. It would properly not be a good idea to buy lots of cold cuts because many of our neighbors were vegetarians. Tofu? Rennet-less cheese? This territory is a minefield of political correctness! If you brought in a kettle full of hot dogs (composed of what?), or only offered hamburgers (the slaughterhouse is cruel and ought to be shut down were it not for big business clout), or if you offered potato chips from one of the multi-national conglomerates (do you favor the multi-nationals in everything you buy? Don't you realize the effect they are having on the environment?), you would be scowled at. The more I thought about the upcoming party, the more glad I was that I would be gone. And so I left, and the next day the block party was held.

Upon my return I asked my wife about the party: was it fun?, had anyone criticized the food or drink? She said that it had been pretty good and that she had met many new neighbors. But she did say that one woman came up to her and said, "Where is your partner?"

"You mean my husband?"

"Oh, I see, you are not a lesbian. That's OK."

My wife explained that I was in New York state, at a small town upstate taking a hunter's safety course. This woman then asked, "Does he own guns? Does he beat you up?" Then, my wife excused herself to show a few small children the location of the bathroom.

In later years I was able to attend the block party. At first I looked forward to it, and enjoyed it. But what struck me after awhile is this: there was no connection between the block party and the rest of the year. It led to a few dinner parties, no more waves, perhaps even <u>less</u> acknowledgment. How has our society become so unfriendly, by what small incipient steps? Once our politics and religion were ferreted out (not hard to do since we were both outspoken), we felt less a part of the club that ought to be any neighborhood.

Today, everyone is touchy, too touchy, myself included. I can remember 50 years ago parties that my folks had, big parties with lots of beer and Scotch, hard drinks of all kinds, since this was before the "discovery" of Chardonnay. I remember always going to the bathroom and surprising some strange woman on the john: she had not locked the door and there was her thigh, long and white, at which I might delightfully stare.

Always there would be arguments, huge arguments. Everybody would be yelling, gesticulating, speaking practically at the same time. It would be heated, intense. But, no one ever got mad. And then, someone would holler out, "Where's the damn beer?," and there would be laughter, lots of laughter. And then, finally the ethnic jokes would start, first with jokes about the Poles, and then, all the other groups: the Irish, the Italians, the Puerto Ricans, the Jews, everybody! They would tell nasty, funny, obscene hilarious, raunchy jokes about every group in the world, and then they would start all over again. Some of the people, both men and woman, would be laughing so hard they would have to leave the room, so as not to wet themselves, or as my mom would say, "not to piss themselves up." I laughed at all the jokes even if I didn't understand them completely, and eventually everyone would be laughing, laughing contagiously for hours it seemed, until, finally, the supply of Scotch ran out or the last ice cube melted, or somebody made an unseemly pass at someone else's wife until the husband said: "Knock it off, Ralph!." Those were proper parties! Why can't we have them again? Is it because everyone has to pass a political correctness test before they get invited?

CHAPTER SIX:
Cheasters

"Cheasters" is not in the proper dictionary: I just looked! (Did you know that "cheasters" is a slang word for spectacles: The endless variety of language!) But, it is easy to guess what the word means: those that only go to Church on Christmas and Easter. The only logical reason for not attending Mass for 50 out of 52 Sundays must be that the person does not regard the spiritual life as important, something to be worked at like golf or a foreign language.

Many years ago in religion class we were made to feel guilty if, as Catholics, we missed Mass. Indeed, we were told that to do so was a sin. Were these nuns' admonitions inaccurate? Does sin still exist or has it gone away like the dodo bird or 13 cents a gallon gasoline? If sin does not exist how is immoral behavior possible, or are all actions ethically equal?

Today, in Rome, 7% of Romans attend Sunday Mass. All over Europe, but most particularly in France and Holland, churches are shuttered. In England where we lived for a time, the Church (there the Church of England, or C of E) is a place where people go for baptisms, weddings and funerals, and other than that, attendance is very low. There, the Church plays more of a social, not religious, role. Is this a good thing? What will happen to our society if this trend continues or grows even larger?

Some secular progressives like, for example, Bill Maher (born an Irish Catholic like me, he now daily mocks the faith), commonly blame religion for wars, all kinds of "hang-ups" including sexual, adolescent unhappiness, stunted humanity, etc. Some of these people, I think it is fair to say, actually hate religion, and many, aided by the ACLU, have attempted in many cases successfully to remove any reference to religion from society: my children cannot pray aloud in school, whereas, had I gone to a public school back in the 50s and 60 prayer would have been accepted as part of a normal curriculum.

Routinely, especially in places like Vermont, religion is made fun of. We are told that to nurture a faith is to be a square. Some analysts say that it is better for a child of, say, ten years to be able to choose a faith, rather than have it forced upon them.

Many of us, especially in our 20s and 30s, leave the faith. Somehow it loses its freshness: this is another way of saying that we no longer are working on it. Like any muscle not used, after but a brief time, faith will shrink.

I believe it is fair to say that my brother for many years ignored his faith, at least by all outward appearances. He was your normal lapsed Catholic. Then, one day aged 61, he was diagnosed with pancreatic cancer. Overnight, God became important. He began once again to go to mass, to speak with priests, to pray. It is good that God gave to him those six months before his death to prepare for his next voyage home. He could easily have been hit by a car and killed instantly; then, there would have been no time for preparation.

In our town in Vermont, huge attendance for Midnight Christmas Mass takes place. So many people wish to attend that a large local hall must be used: the regular small church is far too small. Parents bring all their children and everyone arrives early and is dressed in their best clothing. Yet, the next Sunday after Christmas has passed, the small church is once again plenty large for the small congregation.

I think what we are dealing with here is this: first, people do not think that the spiritual life is <u>that</u> important, and second, people generally feel that the commandment to attend Mass is a <u>suggestion</u> and not a rule. Thus, one hears the phrase "cafeteria Catholic," whereby, like in a cafeteria line, one can pick and choose what rules to follow, to which tenets one ought to adhere.

Obedience to a dictum: in my youth that was a prerequisite for a Christian life. Now the word itself has nearly disappeared! How infrequently it is heard!

We are, of course, engaged in a long-term social experiment: What will happen to a society which largely eschews faith? What will replace it to hold together society's fraying threads? Absent a clearly defined set of rules, reverenced and respected, how does one know which rule to follow? Is it peer pressure or social mores or perhaps waves of always moving desire that is to be the director of one's soul? And don't our desires always shift, move, alter? As children, we crave a mother's smell and a rubber ducky. Then we want a blue sting ray bike. Next as men we lust after a soft breast or curved calf. Adulthood engenders a thirst for cash and then middle age brings with it, a concern for steady health: am I well? Finally, as the body begins to ebb away, we search for that rubber ducky again and, perhaps, the scent of a daughter charged with our care. I can smell her nearby as once I smelled my mother: she is making for me my favorite torta di ciliege and bringing to me my special glass of Terran. But the point in this: absent a Deity and the rules He proposes, how can the cheasters lead a steady and faithful life, if their boat is only buoyed by these constantly shifting, always moving, forever altering desires?

In this contest, Vermont is the crucible. A trial or test is going on there wherein for many if not all religion has been replaced by political or social beliefs, by socialism, by the gay agenda, by yoga, by extreme environmentalism, by Pilates, by technology, by whatever force or factor a person may strongly adopt. This experiment is being carried out today, right under our noses. Initial results are not encouraging, in my view: for one thing non-religious people tent to be more unhappy (Read William Donahue of the Catholic League and especially its journal <u>Catalyst</u>, Volume 35, Number 5. June 2008.) . And for another, faith has been replaced by a non-religion, say extreme environmentalism, which is really nothing more than a set of social/ scientific beliefs: it is <u>not</u> a religion and, therefore, cannot be expected to do the things that a religion can do: bring one closer to God or find peace.

Thus, the gay person who pursues that course as if it were

a religion will be disappointed, no matter how thoroughly he surrounds himself with the like-minded. It is a bit like trying to catch a fish with a baseball bat: the net will always be empty.

Most of these Vermont parents would have inherited their religion as one assumes a father's lambswool sport coat. Faith, however, to be strong must be achieved or earned. Obviously, most of these cheaters see little or no need for a vigorous faith. At some point, they must have rejected both God and the wishes of their parents. Is it not a scary thing to reject God, to tell Him resolutely to go to Hell. How can one be so sure that He is dead? But, so great is our culture of the self, of the primacy of the individual, that that rejection was made possible. Does it not bespeak arrogance, to contravene one's parents, to so belittle a Deity? Socrates said that the fundamental question is: To what extent ought I to be humble? I do not think he would today be pleased.

They say, "I do not wish someone telling me what to do. I will not be subservient to an unseen dogmatic God. I want to pursue my own course!" My parents, on the other hand, tested by the Depression and World War II, saw God as a friend who might help them though difficult times. Difficulties strengthen faith; suffering brings improvement. The death of a child (as happened to them: their eldest daughter was aged 5 when she succumbed to leukemia) makes clear the necessity of faith.

But today's generation, raised on the toxic notion that if I am happy, the world is happy, has had an easy time of it. They calculate, poorly, that if problems arise in the future, say an illness or financial distress, then and only them, will God be consulted. Until then He is not on the stage; he is simply ignored.

However, faith is like a motorcycle: if it sits unused in the garage, the battery will soon die. Faith needs to be tended, nurtured, worked.

One of my favorite uncles, I think it is again fair to say, avoided religion: it was for the other guy. Then, towards the end of his life, with his knees shot, his eyesight very poor, his heart failing, he called me and asked for help or strength. I told him that he probably needed to pray. He said, "I don't know how to begin." I said, "Speak to Him as if He were your best friend. And begin immediately: start."

Discussing the willful rejection of a deity and at the same time (since that lacuna must be filled) an embrace of moral relativism (what desire will chart my progress today?), it is fitting to end this chapter by quoting St. Paul, who was on his way to attack the Christians until he fell off the donkey: and there and then he had a vision, for at last to see. He believed that varying moral standards are a prescription for endless wandering and unhappiness. In the second book of Letters to Timothy (3: 1-5), St. Paul writes:

"Understand this: there will be terrifying times in the last days. People will be self-centered and lovers of money, proud, haughty, abusive, disobedient to their parents, ungrateful, irreligious, callous, implacable, slanderous, licentious, brutal, hating what is good, traitors, reckless, conceited, loves of pleasure rather than lovers of God, as they make a pretense of but deny its power."

CHAPTER SEVEN:
Property Taxes Plus Rebate

When we moved to the Green Mountain state I the summer of 2002, I recall looking at our property tax bill of $5000 and saying to myself that it was too high. Little did I know that within five years it would rise to $16,000. "Where's the gin?," I would ask, "Where's the gin? Somebody make me a giant, ice-cold cocktail, please!"

These very expensive public schools must be paid for somehow. I am of the contrary and cranky opinion that a child's performance is not necessarily proportional to spending. Teachers, liberals, progressives, whatever moniker is preferred, would have us believe in the following graph that m=1 as shown in Table #1 below.

Table #1

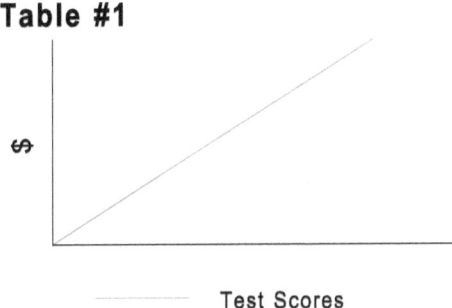

Test Scores

or, in other words, that the more money, teachers, aides, supplements, etc., that you offer to a student, the higher his grades will be. I believe the graph ought to be a bell curve displayed in Table #2.

Table #2

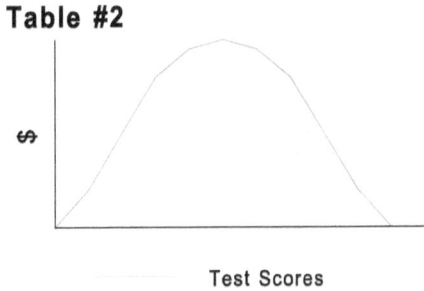

Test Scores

This shows that here is an optimum spending level per student and that past that spending level, performance drops precipitously. I sent this, I believe to be accurate, analysis to the superintendent of schools in Vermont: funny, I did not get a response!

A few years back, a small panel of Vermont judges decided that every school district had to have level spending, and that it was intrinsically unfair for richer towns to have better schools. Thus, money from our wealthy district goes to poorer districts. I do not think that this scheme is generally popular across the United States, but in Vermont, always now verging on socialism (re: redistribution of wealth) it was accepted by most Vermonters with barely a shrug or whimper. In the old days, before this type of social engineering became so popular, the state capitol, Montpelier, parents would search out the better school districts for their children and simply move there. Now, the schools all are, at least on the surface of things, equal and <u>very</u> well funded.

One day maybe six months after our arrival, I was complaining to one of our neighbors about our $5000 tax bill. (This was before the more-than-three-fold increase!) He said that his bill was $3000 but that, because of state rebates, it was actually $2000. "How is that?," I asked plaintively. He said, "The state gives me a break because I am low income. Mary and I have chosen to be poor." Now, getting more than slightly steamed, I asked, "Who picks up the $1000 credit difference? Me or anyone else who pays the full boat!" I walked away before I lost my growing temper and began to muse about how something like this, a Robin Hood idea if there ever were one, could ever have gotten started.

Just the other day Vermont came out with a new program: if you filled out your rebate application incorrectly, Vermont will help you complete it properly even if the date by which the application is meant to be returned has passed: So great is Vermont's willingness to make another handout!

This rebate system helps get school budgets passed. If

"someone who has chosen to be poor" knows that he will not be paying his full share of property taxes, that person is much more likely to vote to approve. Thus, the teachers and the social engineers in Montpelier work hand-in-hand.

This rebate system is rife with fraud, as is any means testing formula. Who can ever know if a rebate application is true? Do we wish to hire thousands of investigators to verify each application? What is to stop a wealthy person from putting his lakeside house in his ne'er-do-well son's name? Where is the uproar about this dishonesty? Where are the calls in the state's main newspaper for investigation? They are nowhere to be read since the editors of the main Burlington paper are proud socialists, though some might deny it.

Some people move to Vermont because of the rebate system, thus making the burden ever greater for those paying the full rate. This is but one of the unintended consequences this legislation has achieved. Another effect is the downward influence the very high, <u>unrebated</u> taxes has on the value of a home: who can appraise that? Nobody!

Clearly, I disagree with the rebate system. It is a redistribution of wealth, pure and simple: taking from the rich and giving to the poor. Since the first days of the graduated income tax, we have had that on the federal level, but is it necessary or wise to have it apply to a state's property tax as well? Some say yes, including those legislators in Montpelier. Long term, both the high property taxes and the rebate scheme will make Vermont more unaffordable. The good governor, Jim Douglas, has been saying this for years. The poor will depart, the middle class gets squeezed, and the increasingly rich will stay: the "big sort" thus continues. And the disparity in wealth, which this law I suppose was meant to address, actually does the reverse: it grows larger.

Now, if you go to the corner store on a Saturday morning to buy a gallon of milk, the *New York Times* is stacked high behind the counter. Our village is full of transplanted New York City denizens. These are hedge fund managers, bankers, analysts, agents: the well-heeled who crave news from the newspaper they used to read when the lived in the City. To these flat-landers, these new Vermonters, the taxes perhaps do not seem so horrendous because by odious comparison, down in the Big Apple and its environs, they are even worse.

But what about the Old Vermonters, those that used to farm, those that voted for Nixon in 1960, those that want to keep, not give away to the government, a nickel? They do not believe in socialism, which is exactly what the rebate system is. They believe in a social safety net, especially for children, but not for able-bodied college-educated adults who have "chosen to be poor." They believe that if you harm a person's ability to become wealthy, that person will feel less of an incentive to work. They do not espouse victimhood whereby the government must solve every problem. They believe in work and in their right to keep the money made from that work. They believe in frugality and in the idea that they, and not the government, are the best, most suited entity to decide where and how to spend. They, some of them at least, do not fully grasp how thoroughly their states has been taken over by socialist ideas. Is it a Yankee laconic rectitude that has aided this rapid transformation? A coup d'etat has been accomplished right under their noses: 40,000 migrants (if you will) have moved in to a state with only 600,000 people and in less than a generation transformed that society from a groups of independent frugal farmers to a progressive socialistic experiment. Since the old Vermonters are naturally taciturn, restrained, and busy with work, all these changes have happened quite easily. Some say, "Take Back Vermont," the opposite spin to what the flatlanders pronounce, "Take Vermont Forward." The old Vermonters that I know look to the future with foreboding (What other crazy socialistic schemes are around the corner?), and they regret that so much: the Yankee independence, and the incentive to work and save, the tight neighborhoods where people could speak without prejudging or rancor, has already been lost, perhaps forever, unless strong and convincing words can bend the minds of men.

If it is true that socialism does not work (There is no incentive to work or save) and if it is also true, as John Kennedy said, that "All businessmen are bastards" (they lie, cheat and steal), what are we to do, that is, how is society to be governed? With judicious laws it shall happen, those meant to control the vagaries of wild business, and the coarser natures of man.

CHAPTER EIGHT:
Counter Culture and Gays

Before I was to enter the University of California at Santa Cruz as a junior, I received a note from my college there, advising me to arrive a week early, not to attend classes, but to "form bonds with my fellow kin-group members." I was told that they were to be my new family. Since I had a steady job working among the orange groves and since I had told my boss that I would work for him that extra week, I declined to go to school early.

The week passed. When I eventually showed up, I was told to go to the dome, a large, white canvas geodesic dome and as I entered a large man, bearded and wearing a flowing kaftan, said to me something like this: "Why did you not show up last week to meet your new family?" I explained that I had given my word to my orange orchard manager/boss and that I already had a very good family with nice parents and lots of brothers and sisters and, therefore, why would I need another? He glared a little and said, "Do I detect resentment?"

"No, not a bit, sir," I said and then sat down directly on the floor, my long legs akimbo, as if I were an Indian or a citizen of Montagnard. I felt the stare of many upon my neck.

Now that many years have passed since that day in 1971, I understand what the large bearded man was saying: "Give up your regular family. Adopt ours, this one, this kin-group. We will be better friends. We will not order you around like your father does. We will not fill you with guilt like your church does. It takes a village, this village, a village we will create fresh each day." And thus, at least for me, the counter culture was born.

As I mentioned in the preface, I had transferred from Gonzaga University to UCSC, from a very traditional Catholic school (where after only two years I nearly had a Minor Degree in Theology) to a very liberal state school where traditional religion was constantly mocked. Who else in the world has made this odd quixotic transfer? Most of my fellow students there at Santa Cruz, I soon discovered had rejected notions that I accepted:

1) the concept of sin
2) the existence of good and evil
3) the idea of judgement day
4) the possibility of hell
5) the fact of heaven
6) the entity that is God

Many believed that a person should be free to do whatever he wants, that, for example, all drug laws are foolish and ought to be rescinded. Moral relativism was everywhere: "Such and such may be acceptable to you but it is disagreeable (or a joke, or to be laughed at) to me, so don't force your stupid backward ways on me. We have moved on, if you haven't!" Too, I understood quickly and much to my lusting chagrin that that first week that I had missed, when the kin-group was establishing my new family, that that time had served as an intense and compact week of mating, sexual pairing up (in various combinations many of which were foreign to me) and that I was "out of the loop," a bit alone, what we used to call a "5th wheel."

Many of my classmates then, thought that they could make up the rules as they went along: shifting desires make for shifting action. They rejected strongly that an outside God of some sort might make rules that were immutable and must be obeyed. To them, the whole idea of commandments was nearly laughable. Indeed, the recently deceased comedian George Carlin, raised an Irish Catholic like I, produced a skit called: "Why We Don't Need Ten Commandments." His anti-religious stance is not unusual in Hollywood. (I will not say that he was a lapsed Catholic: that is not my place. Perhaps, during the heart attack that killed him he had the chance to speak with Someone larger than himself.)

Not long afterward I went to a party at another apartment in our complex. It was a Friday night and the place was packed with people. I grabbed a beer and started to nurse it. Off in the corner, but under bright lights so that all could see, a couple was necking hard; the girl, I noticed, had lovely reddish brown hair that had just been carefully washed and coiffed: it hung half way down her back. I took another sip on my beer and munched on my celery stick. (Rarely was there meat at these gatherings. Lots of lentils, bean dip, and eggplant ratatouille.) Then, the couple concluded their ardent clinch and when the girl turned away from her friend to face me and the rest of the party I saw, to my surprise, that she was a man, not a woman, but a man wearing a growing smile.

Given my sheltered childhood this scene was a bit of a shock, something seminal that one remembers. Ben, for let us call him that, had thrown away traditional standards of sexuality. He had embraced an alternative, and given the smile, apparently happily so. But what are the long term consequences of this action?

One of my nephews a few years later attended the University of San Francisco, another venerable Jesuit institution, and later, over a glass of wine, I asked him, as many goading, teasing uncles might, whether he had become homosexual, given the obvious fact that he had just spent four years in the least heterosexual city in America. Immediately, he chastised me, saying, "You are homophobic. You are a dinosaur!"

"No," I said. "Phobia implies fear. I am not afraid of them. I do not like what they do."

From that point onward, the conversation deteriorated markedly.

What has happened in my lifetime is this: homosexuality in many circles has become normal. For some it is simply a choice with no moral overtones. It is like going to an ice cream stand and asking for blueberry instead of chocolate. The mainstream press generally has given this normalization an easy pass, if not overt encouragement. Now gay couples may marry, adopt and engage in artificial insemination to produce a child. Today in public school my first grade daughter is told that all families are equal, regardless of whether we speak of two daddies, two mommies, or any other combination, as long as there is love. This doctrine of diversity is represented by the rainbow sticker or flag and it is seen all over Vermont as a symbol of acceptance and political correctness.

Civil unions, pairing up two gay people, are now legal in Vermont; this statute was engineered by a small judicial panel and an acquiescent Governor Howard Dean. Never was the issue put up to a vote of all Vermonters. The same clever and premeditated tactic is now being used in many other states across the country: find activist judges and do not put it to a vote. This normalization of gayness has now spread to roughly seven "blue" states. In most, if not all cases, these new laws have been engendered not by the will of the people through a plebiscite, but my activist liberal judges and spineless governors. But, what is wrong with all this? Why am I so worried? Is this not progress? Are not these people entitled to equal rights?

If one accepts the commandments there is not one version that says for me to take a man as a partner. Does the Bible say anywhere that is acceptable to pair up with one of the same sex? Of course, if one rejects the commandments and the Bible as true, this preventative reasoning goes away and one can do as one pleases, as one desires. Desire is the key. Is it to be controlled? Is it to be guarded? Is it to be grown? Does desire ever become excessive or unhealthy? The Greeks believed in moderation (or, at least, some of them did for awhile) but do we? So much of American culture can be summed up in this short dialectic: impulse restraint versus impulse release. Are we to monitor and control our desires or are they to manage us? Clearly for some of the extreme gays who practice unsafe sex, regardless of the fear of getting AIDS, desire has become the central element in their lives, how to feed it, how to enjoy it, how to grow it. Some of these extremes gays (40% is the figure in a recent British magazine study of 300 men) don't know their HIV status and do not speak of it to their partners. Is this not a case where desire rules men and not the other way around?

My view is that these moves to normalize homosexuality merely encourage it. I do not believe that is should be encouraged, that it is simply another, equal option. Despite what the amoral press might have us believe, I maintain that the best family is one with one mother and one father and scads of slightly wild kids. There are many in the gay world who will say that virtually any combination of parents – two fathers, two mothers, whatever – is preferable to the traditional family. Can we ask: "Is that advice to be trusted? Does blood count for so little?" What would Germont from Verdi's La Traviata say: "Does my son, who is not my son, ever return?" Despite what the politically correct school teachers say, I think that to stray from this standard is to ask for trouble. What new strange sexual confusion lurks? If every teenager is told that bisexuality is cool, won't a young man after a few unsuccessful dates with the opposite sex, soon cross over? Indeed, why not, if nothing is wrong?

In our culture, sex is clearly over-emphasized. It is used to sell everything from toothpaste to engine oil. Our culture tells us to make it the center of our lives, but really, biologically, it is meant to have a smaller, though still key, role to play.

I feel sorry for teenagers today. If they have lax parents they are told to experiment with sex early on. Even if the parents are strict, public school teachers advise the freshmen and sophomores how to put on a condom. (Read <u>Unprotected; A Campus Psychiatrist Preveals How Political Correctness in her Profession Endangers Every Student</u>. Sentinal, 2006) It is written by Anonymous, M.D., since she was afraid to lose her job. Half the children in this country, indeed, much of Western Europe as well, have no fathers. He is down the road like Johnny Appleseed, Johnny Chapman, perhaps planting more seed. The social, moral, economic implications of this last fact need to be looked at much more carefully before we can say, as so many progressives do, that abstinence is folly.

When the boys come over to date my daughter they will be questioned thoroughly by us regarding intent: "What do you want to happen tonight?" If they do not pass muster, they will be shown the door, all protests notwithstanding.

Through peer pressure of the most severe form, high school girls especially if they lack strong, questioning fathers, engage in risky sexual behavior that may emotionally scar them for life, though this fact is scarcely discussed; the female physical problems that inevitably follow from a slutty adolescence are continually ignored by a liberal press bent on carefree sexual experimentation.

In Vermont, generally speaking, sex is not seen as something sweet, that is part of marriage. It is part of the overall cultural experimentation: new Vermonters, especially, feel that they ought to be able to indulge most every whim, nearly any growing desire. A weekly tabloid produced in Burlington has a personal section proposing various sundry ways that these escalating desires might be scratched or sated. But has not this sexual revolution lead only to greater dissatisfaction, greater divorce, greater endless bed-hopping? When will that fact be recognized and greater temperance employed?

In Vermont, Jessica's Law has not been adopted apparently because some there see a threat in its system designed to protect the weakest amongst us, young girls. Vermont is one of only a handful of states which has rejected this sensible statute; the path to deny has been lead by the left-leaning legislators in Montpelier. Why would they see that law as a threat? Because it seeks, ultimately, to curtail desire and desire is deemed by some new Vermonters as the new ultimate good.

Finally, in Vermont a couple of years ago Judge Cushman gave a very weak 60-day jail sentence to a convicted child molester (He later lengthened it but only after enormous state and nation-wide pressure). This happened because, once again, desire is proclaimed the universal good, no matter toward what end it grows. Desire can only be so elevated, if first, God and his commandments, have been denied. All desires are not equal and any, too long pursued, can slay.

These godless counter cultural hedonistic experiments in Vermont will deliver the results that they intrinsically foretell: numerous peaks and valleys of pleasure and despair, periodic sharp loneliness, near remorse and the predator's tiny riddle, and, more than anything else, a deep morass of sexual confusion which, some maintain, is the worst kind of all.

One final thought: many politicians are resolutely dodging this issue by saying it, the question of whether gay marriage should exist, ought to be left up to the individual states. But what happens to the gay couple, legally married in Massachusetts, who moves to Virginia and then, with the unhappy passage of time, decide to get a divorce? The Commonwealth of Virginia correctly does not allow gay marriage. Therefore, it maintains that it cannot dissolve a union that was never truly formed. In truth, gay marriage must be a federal issue, but should it exist in the first place? Most gay activists know that if the question were put up to a normal vote, it would be properly denied. So, they do an end around, and, once again, another voice is silenced. Do not all have the innate right to speak?

CHAPTER NINE:
Farming Gone

One day while at work at the winery and vineyard in California, the assistant agricultural commissioner or someone close to that position called me and said, "Nick, you have to come in and take a test to spray your vines." I knew him slightly, enough to joke around a little, so, I said instantly, "Cram it. No damn way." and I hung up. He called back immediately (I knew that he would) and said, "You are the third guy in fifteen minutes that has said the same thing."

"Why is that?," I asked him, "why is that?"

Farming suffers from too much regulation. New rules are constantly being added, often made by people who would not know the front end of the tractor from the rear. They think PTO stands for Permanent Tropical Opportunity. In Vermont, soon, I expect, farmers who graze cows will be instructed to fence off all creeks on their land. Despite the fact that **farmers are their own best regulators**, government is always telling them, with threat of fine, what to do, and how to do it.

Today, many Vermont farmers choose subsidies from the federal or state government. Well-financed lobbyists coerce pliant weak legislators to pass new laws adding to the already severely bloated and expensive system of subsidies. What started out many years ago as a <u>temporary</u> bit of assistance has grown to become a permanent socialistic fixture. Where are the market fores? Do not these large subsidies, especially those that are fixed, transmute the market, skew it? Witness today the effect that the federal subsidy for corn for fuel (not for feed, and not for food) has had on the price of corn tortillas! Once again: beware unintended consequences!

There has not been a move to wean ourselves away from the subsidies because the well-healed lobbyists, who give much money to re-election campaigns, will not stand for it; secondly, paralyzed complaint law-makers do not grasp the problem; and third, many farmers have become addicted to all that money which acts as a drug.

I am all for a state promoting itself. Vermont makes wonderful maple syrup (soon to be even more expensive due to the cost of fuel), smoked meats (Dakin Farms near us has the best bacon east of the Mississippi!), and it even has, on southward facing slopes near to Lake Champlain, a fledgling wine business. Attempts are being made in Montpelier to aid the artisan cheese business but to me these programs are too expensive, and what's more, when I go to the cheese section in the grocery store I am always shocked at the very high prices. Should promotions not be best left up to the cheese maker himself or, perhaps, the cheese co-operative to which he belongs?

Good farmers are cheap, resourceful, inventive. They work harder than anyone else, period, and get paid the least. Often all their inputs (tractor, fuel, etc.) are purchased at retail, yet the product they make is sold at wholesale. Why do they continue, those that do? Because they love it; they do not want to be in some office arguing about who is going to brew the coffee.

Vermont used to have thousands of dairies; now there are about 800. Our street itself at one time had five or six; today, none. Part of the problem is the increase in pop, sodas, the dreaded vitamin water, and various so-called health drinks. All dairymen should look at those drinks as the enemy. Milk is one of nature's most perfect foods (along with figs) yet it gets no respect! I'm Irish and therefore slow, but can someone please explain to me how in a dairy state like Vermont , it is still possible to buy pop from vending machines at school but not milk?

One of the other problems facing farmers is the difficulty in finding adequate help. Fifty years ago <u>all</u> high school boys had full-time jobs. Then, the social engineers jumped in and made that impossible. Apples in Vermont are picked by Haitians or Jamaicans; often they are illegal and therefore, they are constantly afraid to leave the ranch. If a people cannot pick its own fruit and vegetables, does that not portend the inevitable demise of that culture?

It used to be that all work had value, however menial. (Wittgenstein changed bed pans.) Now, many kids, say college aged, want to make large amounts of money for little work and though they have no experience. Most farmers would prefer to hire foreigners, even if they are illegal, because they are vastly better workers and do not "talk back." Plus, you do not have to work around their social life.

Millions of dollars have been spent investigating the health, or lack thereof, of Lake Champlain. What a gravy train! The liberal eco newspaper in Burlington usually blames the farm for everything: increased phosphates, nitrates, eutrophication, algae blooms, yet the number of cows is less, not more, and farming practices have much improved over the past 50 years.

Maybe part of the problem is zoning: everyone wants to have five acres in the county. Chittenden County, the home of Burlington and what used to be dozens of small farming villages, is now pretty much a suburb. This was a huge mistake driven my the always-too-powerful real estate interests. No farmer is going to farm three acres here, four acres there: it is not worth his bother! If he tried, the new neighbors just up from Westchester County would probably complain about the dust or noise or early working hours or something. In Europe, they have it right: they protect agricultural land between towns; it is not subdivided, or built upon. They understand that the land is their future and they cluster homes in already existing towns. All across America one can see this wasteful and ugly sprawl.

The worst incidence of this, in my view, took place not in Vermont but on the Oxnard plain of California. There, the black, rich, topsoil is 20 or 30 feet thick. Anything, more or less, can be grown. When I was in highschool, I would go down there to get tractor pasts for my boss. The ranches were pristine, well-tended usually by Japanese, and the crops were bountiful. The problem was these productive ranches were too close to the crawling behemoth: Los Angeles. Throughout the exuberant 70s and 80s, the ranches were sold and subdivided; box stores, dozens and dozens, along with huge housing tracts were built and now cover the rich topsoil. Yes, there are still some vegetable farms (where you can get over-large, tasteless strawberries all year round), but it is not like it used to be.

Speaking of which, why do we expect to be able to buy strawberries at any time. Aren't they a seasonal crop?? Most of our buying options are based upon fuel at $1.00 per gallon. Such bounty now, for the moment, exists. Many new Vermonters have become slaves to the notion that "I should be able to buy watermelon in December, spinach in July, asparagus in the Fall, and grapes in the Spring." Do they not know that grapes purchased in the Spring probably come from Chile? The produce section in most Vermont stores (as well as those across the country) is grossly over-stocked with out-of-season, probably tasteless, fruits and vegetables; and much of the purchase price is shipping. As we climb towards $5.00 per gallon, maybe we ought to begin to re-think what we purchase and when. Does anyone ever stop to think that God gave us citrus to eat in the Winter, to prevent scurvy, and that he surrounded those fruits with a thick, long-lasting skin?

We should use as our model the Europeans. In our local fruit and vegetable shop in Crewkerne, Somerset, the selection was paltry but it was all very fresh and very local. In the winter it was mostly potatoes, swedes, turnips, beets, but we came to enjoy them. Soon it was Spring and we would switch to the stone fruits (obst). And so on. There was a natural rhythm that was satisfying. Can Americans, so long used to excessive choice, learn to adapt to a more restricted set of choices?

Many new Vermonters, having moved to the Green Mountain State, immediately start telling the Vermont farmer how to farm, what sprays to (not) use, how much fertilizer is just the right amount. They push equally neophyte legislators in Montpelier for increasingly restrictive statutes regarding exactly how to farm. Such arrogance! Many are very quick to blame the farmer for <u>any</u> purported pollution in Lake Champlain, blaming the farmer for over-fertilization. (But wait-a-minute! Isn't the farmer frugal? Why would he over-fertilize?) At work here is anti-farmer animus based not on his polluting but on the fact that he is a capitalist, that he wants to make and keep a profit. If there is a dirty word left in Vermont today, it is that one: capitalist!

A simple way to fix the lake, which may or may not be suffering from excess phosphates and nitrogenous compounds, is to get rid of all causeways: they obstruct the ebb and flow of the water and thus lead to anaerobic conditions and eutrophication. Stop spending millions every years on useless, inconclusive studies and build bridges instead of causeways. Next question!

One day a local, large landholder (read: capitalist interested in a profit) proposed a 1500 head cow operation nearby. Within days the campaign against him was joined. Parents at the Little League games of my son wore t-shirts that read:

"Concerned Citizens Who Wish to Protect Agriculture." Those t-shirts, if more truthful, might have read "Nervous Whingers Who Don't Want to Smell Cow Poo." Eventually, the large land-owner postponed his project. That way, the new Vermonters can continue to get their beef (if they eat it!) from Georgia, and their chicken from Arkansas. But, think of all those truck miles! Where is the ecology in that?

CHAPTER TEN:
Anti-Catholic

Historically, Vermont has long been a strongly Catholic states. Most of the small towns that dot the Green Mountains have a Catholic church, though many, because of a sharp decline in vocations, no longer have a diocesan priest assigned to them, at least individually. It is my contention that, that fact and any other fact that points toward the Church's decline, pleases many who reside in the state. But, why would they care?

If a Church exists and thrives, saying that heaven, sin and judgement exist, and a secular humanist believes the opposite, the Church will be viewed as a hostile entity, an enemy to be met and possibly defeated. That sort of battle is raging in Vermont today.

The battle is waged in the press, in community halls, in town squares and at the grocery store. Public schools now teach young children that all families, however constructed, are equal, contrary to Church doctrine. Civil unions, supposedly uniting two homosexuals in a <u>faux</u> marriage, flaunt the rule of the Church. Drug laws are continually weakened or not rigorously enforced, causing untold damage to body and mind, but these non-actions are given the culture's blanket imprimatur which says it's a good thing to "turn on." Schools, and some liberal parents, encourage their children to experiment with all sorts of premarital sex, disregarding the Church's teaching and the possible medical and emotional damage those fun sprees may possibly cause.

Many liberal parents in Vermont treat their children like they would a college buddy. Sternness and obedience are diminished. The dictatorial father who wishes to be minded is made fun of and marginalized by, say, the two gay women, both of whom nurture and protect, rather than instruct and insist.

Most of these general statements, if not all, do not apply to old Vermonters, who are as normal as parents anywhere in the country: they worry about what uncontrolled bad things: drugs, sex, alcohol, etc., may happen to their children. They teach by example, they instigate discussion at the dinner table and, if necessary, they are emphatic or very clear. But, in Vermont, that model of parenting is slipping away, replaced by the new Vermonters' laissez-faire.

Radical parents do not chastize; they do not insist on a particular religion, or one at all. Some, perhaps because <u>they</u> did it back in the wild 60s and 70s, encourage experimentation with drugs, sex, and alcohol. They say, "Release that impulse. Do not be inhibited. You just have to keep it under control." How different this lackadaisical mode is from my upbringing where my nurturing and kind mother gave the orders and my stern and laconic father was around the corner to make sure they were enforced and to raise his strong sailors' voice if required.

The public school is the primary vehicle through which many of these cultural and moral changes can be implemented. How easy, if not facile, has been the metamorphosis! (Is there not a spot of derision included?) Since all religion has, more or less, with the help of the ACLU and activist (read: liberal) judges, been excluded from the school, we are powerless, there , to protest the very early sex education, the lax drug policies, the weak smoking standards, the complacent attitudes towards alcohol and, most importantly, the agenda of diversity, normalizing homosexuality and refuting hundred of years of Church teachings.

Where are the parents in all of this? New Vermonters tend to think one way, and old Vermonters the other. Many traditional parents, I would bet, are intimidated by the very liberal agenda, the endless political correctedness, put in place in the schools by teachers and administrators who, it cannot be debated, are distinctly more liberal than the population as a whole. They think: "Do not rock the boat," and perhaps by temperament - that Yankee rectitude and quiet forbearance - they are somewhat frozen or paralyzed.

One February evening I went over to the local public school to play basketball in a men's league. It was Black History Month and in the hallway outside the gym there were 15 or so large displays touting Martin Luther King, Jr., W. E. B. Dubois, and the like: the black heroes in the cause of civil rights. I said to myself, "Fine. That is part of history." But, then, down at the end of the hall, I saw I couple of placards: one devoted to the Black Panthers and one based on H. Rap Brown and Stokely Carmichael. Those two displays spoke about how these men were men of non-violence, but that was not true! They did not deserve to be part of the Black History, but who wants to protest this to the left-leaning principal; who wants to rock the boat; who wants to be seen as someone "uncool?" Thus, and shortly, history is transmuted and transposed.

Whenever I went to one of our kids' games and tried to strike up a conversation, people would say, "I've never seen you at the school." I would reply that "we send our kinds to a Catholic school so that they can get some sort of religious education." I would not seek to persaude or proselytize, that much I promise. Often then and not always, I would get a strong look that said, " you've got two heads," and the conversation, though just started, would be over. I had crossed a line, the line which states that the school (not the Church) is sacrosanct.

Eventually, to stir things up some more (Why not? I was raised by my folks to always ask the difficult question), at those ballfields and baseball diamonds, I would mention how the property taxes, fueling wastefully the anti-religious schools, have risen at a rate well above inflation for years, and what do you think of that? Then, quickly, I would either have made a new friend or pissed off fully a disgruntled liberal. Ha!

Soon, I noticed that the daily newspaper in Burlington near us seemed to have a clear and consistent Anti-Catholic bias. There would be long stories about molestation cases.

Now, let me say this: priests that molest young men or women have committed a despicable crime, one which causes great harm, one for which they will have to pay considerable penance. I feel sorry and pray for those victims. Too many times the Church tried to push the matter under the carpet. But those days are gone. The Church has confronted, finally, the issues with charity and transparency. But the newspaper coverage implies that the Church has done little and that it encourages bad priests. More than anything, it encourages settlement amounts again the Church that are way beyond the window of fairness, and not even close to an appropriate penalty for these painful crimes.

Why do these arch liberals desire such high settlement amounts? Because I believe that they wish the Church to go under, these rote progressives anticipate that she will have to sell off all her assets to pay the bill, and finally they hope that the Catholic parishioners, seeing all of this, will be disgusted and attendance will drop to zero and the churches will close. I believe that this is the goal of the secular humanist, these wing-nut new Vermonters: to have religion disappear, to be replaced by a motley construct of cultural and political ideas left over from the Sixties, trends including but not limited to, the following: socialism, extreme environmentalism, sexuality unconstrained by traditional morality, controlled drug use and sissified victimology. That is what happens when a small state of only 600,000 people, hard-working, frugal people, who wish mostly to be left along, is invaded by, say, 30,000 aging hippies who were once told they were the smartest generation ever. Are they or do they only think it so? Now they feel entitled, embittered; they are disinclined to work; they wonder, surrounded by divorce, how has the sexual revolution failed them? They are always telling someone else what to do and how to think; they do not wish to debate and do not know how to laugh. Maybe they are not so smart after all. Surely they are not the best generation! That would have been comprised of their parents who probably look down from on high upon this strange tableau and can only groan, only groan.

I would be strangely and strongly remiss, finally, if I did not discuss the fact that since <u>Roe v. Wade</u> in 1973, 45 million babies have been aborted. Will this be the central legacy of my coddled generation, the idea that because it is "inconvenient" destruction of a perfectly healthy baby is justified? Maybe if members of my generation had not hopped from mattress to mattress like so many fornicating and mindless rabbits those "procedures" would not have been necessary. The radial left is always saying that we need more sex education in the public school to prevent an unwanted pregnancy. What a load of rubbish! What we need is for teenagers, or those in their 20s and 30s who act like teenagers (Read Diana West's <u>The Death of the Grown-Up</u>. New York: St. Martin's Press, 2007) to stop taking their clothes off in front of each other; how can they "be surprised" when the biological urge takes over? I remember with glee how Governor Deukemajian of California noted the <u>increase</u> in unwed mothers after years of always increasing state wide sex education. He said that he sex education was having a <u>pro</u>- pregnancy effect and in the last days of his term, ever the contrarian, he cut the spending.

The sexual revolution has produced divorce and disquietude, and feminism has delivered castrated fathers and ready abortion: what a sad vestige! Daily, the Catholic Church, adhering to a doctrine of life, fights this cancer on our society. Some left extremists, both men and women, see available abortion as something almost "holy" or "sacramental" in their canon of a proper life, a "divine right," and something to which all women are entitled. There's that word again: entitled. But, what about the child inside, breathing, feeling, thinking? A society is graded by how it treats the most powerless, its weakest citizens: do they not qualify?

The next death – embracing frontier is euthanasia: the right and ability for someone who is sick or infirm to end his own life by a switch of a valve, or the turn of a screw. This, sometimes, is not God's intention. Sometimes we are meant to suffer. Some say that it is only through suffering that one can improve or cleanse one's soul. Oregon, a state similar to Vermont in its counter-culture demographic, recently posed a very liberal "right-to-die" bill. I predict that similar misguided laws will be proposed in many more of the blue states where, since they defy God's will, they have quickly been adopted by the radical left as another part of their anti-life candor or mantras. Kill babies, kill old people who no longer get a kick out of life.

Once again and arrogantly, people try to place themselves as more powerful than God. The whole idea of obedience to His rules or that we must bow before Him to ask for direction or forgiveness, has been lost and replaced by death's cold embrace, rather than life's affirmation.

This is not a pretty picture, when people so affront a god,

so willingly and gladly seek his dismissal. We must ask: what happens to a society, like Vermont's, that proposes and follows these anti-religious, secular values? What occurs to that culture if that course is long pursued? Let me pose the answer that I see this way: when we lived through those quickly passing 5 years, always I used to comment to my wife how few smiling bright faces I had seen that day. People there are disproportionately grim, though they might not see it so. They have abandoned religion and yet have found no other calm or succor. Drastically, they scratch and seek, look and long. Yet God, whom they have renounced, says: "If you follow My commandments, you will find peace." Having dismissed the king, they are unlikely to follow his dicta. God was always there nearby, but I had not seen Him, or so said Goethe: "Mehr Licht!" on his deathbed"; "More light!"

I ought to conclude on a mildly confessional note: I used to be like them, these a religious intransigents. That is how and why I may be able to describe them so accurately. After all, we went to the same schools, had the same teachers, and read the same books. In those days, I, too, thought little of God; I disregarded Him. I cared little for the commandments, the possibility of Judgement Day or the afterlife. I was concerned only with my own pleasure and the accumulation of money, as were so many of my compatriots. Yes, I, too, was a moral relativist!

Then, as happens, my life changed or sadly turned. Soon after, I met a woman who made me laugh again (and, perhaps, vice versa.) Nine months later, after our quick marriage, a son appeared and I can still recall the sharp pang of emotion when

I saw for the 1ˢᵗ time his frail shoulders. (I need to nod deeply here to James Joyce and his short poem "On the Beach at Fontana." James Joyce: <u>Poems</u> <u>and</u> <u>Shorter</u> <u>Writings</u>. New York: Faber and Faber, 1991) Shall I say "trembling fine boned… and his boyish arm"? Instantly a life changed or turned again, but, this time, happily so. And there it is: Eureka! I have found it, the small truth, the tender nugget: children bring us back to God.

Afterwards, I no longer thought so much of my own pleasure or of money. These topics seemed to me small. I wondered for the 1ˢᵗ time how to be a good father, with what words I should address them. Instantly, I knew that this job: to be a good father to our now three children would be my most important task. Instinctively, I asked God for His advice and paid no heed to the scattered catcalls of derision all around.

CHAPTER ELEVEN:
A Library Intruder

One evening, enjoying a cocktail as is our wont, perhaps a Gimlet or Blue Lady, I mentioned to my wife the old joke that cars in Vermont won't start unless the cell phone is on. Ha! Though the state be green, the reliance on technology daily grows.

My wife said that a representative of our electrical company had come by to ask our opinion of the transmission line upgrade that it proposed. The power poles on our street dated back to 1939. The electrical company wanted to replace then with new, slightly taller ones. My wife said: "Electricity? Electricity? Do what you want. Do I look like someone who can explain electricity? I can't even tell you how the can-opener works." (Thank you, Woody Allen.) The rep said that he felt faint and asked if he could sit down and have a glass of water. Ha! Later, when he improved a little, he said that her common sense response was the first of its kind all day: frequently he had been lambasted by wild-eyed homeowners for fouling the environment, or lectured on the intricacies of electrical transmission by people who had learned about it from obscure and untrustworthy websites.

I recalled to my wife the freezing January morning when one of our box elder trees had split, downing a power line and knocking out the power in the neighborhood. It was Christmas time, relatives would be visiting, most homeowners had given up their generators in the unconstrained push towards suburbia, and, all in all I felt guilty. I brought out some hot coffee for the linemen trying to reestablish the power. As soon as I got there, a large black SUV stopped (the driver shutting off the ubiquitous cell phone) and he, with no preamble, asked, "When will the power be back on?" Not, "Merry Christmas!" or "Pretty damn cold today; sorry you're out here." But, "what can you do for me?" He drove off in a huff and I could see that he was back on his cell phone before you could say 'Connecticut River Valley.'

I watched the lineman's slightly frowning face and said, emphatically: "Jerk!"

"Ah, hell," he said, "don't worry 'bout it. He's just another flat-lander who is impatient and likes to complain. He thinks this whole area is his own personal park. He doesn't get it: we have electricity to deliver! Yet, he is the first to complain. These telephone poles are more than 40 years old; they are 20 feet too short. But the new Vermonters like the rustic look. Thanks for the coffee. I better get back to work, else my boss will have my ass in a sling." I told my wife that that scene was a perfect microcosm for the inherent conflict between old and new Vermonters, and she told me to be quiet and pour her another splash of the Blue Lady.

About that same time the 2004 election neared. We had placed, prominently, a Bush sign in our driveway. It could be seen by anyone driving up and down the street. It was one of the few in the neighborhood but we didn't care: we believed in the Iraq war, that Bush had to be firm, not a wet dish-rag in fighting terrorism and that Saddam Hussein had defied the United Nations and the world by not complying with the truce from the first Iraq war. Howard Dean was running for President and the Democratic party under his coercion and persuasion was shifting sharply, always further left. To gain political advantage much of the country turned. Democrats who had not too long ago approved the war now opposed it, and rebuked Bush endlessly, calling him a liar and a dunce. The largely liberal media parroted these ideas and almost seemed to display the very difficult scenes in Bagdad with glee, so much did they wish for, or so it seemed, an American defeat (Read David Horowitz and Ben Johnson's The Party of Defeat. Dallas: Spence Publication Company, 2008). Whatever happened to American unity, the kind we displayed, for example, in World War II?

But, all of that, for the purpose of this discussion, is besides the point: should we not be able to express our viewpoint freely? Why did I notice around our area increased glares directed towards us? Whatever happened to the America where opinions could be exchanged without rancor or animosity?

The next night, while I was explaining to my wife, my new rule: Dominic's theorem: that anyone with more than 4 bumper stickers on their car is crazy, the phone rang. It was a policeman with an Irish surname and a very friendly manner and he asked if he could come over to see me the next night at 5 pm. I said "Sure. Would you like a whiskey?"

So, the next night (since my wife was gone) I told our 3 kids that a policeman would be coming over to have a talk with me. My son said, "Will he be packing heat?" Our youngest wondered, "What did you do wrong, daddy?" The oldest said, "You must have done something wrong or else he would not be wasting his time." The doorbell rang and I gulped.

He was very short. He looked at me and said "Hello, Mr. Martin. You're pretty tall. How tall are you?" I said that I was between six foot two or six foot three. "What's this about?," I asked. We moved into the parlor.

He related how a couple of nights previous, a man about my age and sporting a face, sadly, a bit like mine, had entered the town library near to closing time. He had hid in the men's room and pretended not to hear the admonition from the lone librarian to leave the building since the library was about to close. Then, coming up behind the older women seated at her computer, he attached her, grabbing at her necklace. She screamed and he thankfully became frightened and scampered off. Understandably, she was quite frightened and reported the incident to the police.

As the policeman told this tale, I was thinking I had heard that they were looking for this pervert, but that he was five foot nine inches and very overweight. (This overweight business hurt my vanity. The children are always calling me Signor

Panza, Mr. Stomach.) So, I asked him, "Why are you visiting me when I am nearly six inches taller than this creep?"

"I know, I know," he said," but I have to follow up on all leads; somebody fingered you."

"Who?," I said point-blank. He looked at me like we were just two guys at a bar arguing about a football team: Notre Dame is better than USC, that sort of thing. For a moment there I understood that he wanted to tell me the name, but his good police training stopped him. He only said, "She is someone in the neighborhood," and then he left. Always he had been polite, almost kind. Maybe someday soon I'll see him in a bar and buy him a drink, a Rob Roy or Sidecar.

So, the only thing we could conclude from this unamusing scene is that some grim female nearby had seen our Bush sign or heard about our conservative politics and Catholic religion, and said to herself that it would be a good thing to make our life difficult. Given the near half-foot difference in height and the clear and obvious fact that I am not over-weight, what other conclusions may be made?

At first this experience left me feeling a bit spooked or afraid, but after a day or so I became not agitated, but angry, thinking: whatever happened to civil disclosure, the ability for people to have opposing views, in short, tolerance? I remember those wild parties of my parents or exactly 50 years ago when the men and women of our neighborhood, holding Manhattans or Tom Collins in their hands would argue with each other endlessly;, everybody, my mom and dad, the cat, would loudly hold forth on some damn topic, and how then, someone on the edge of the fight would say: "Cram it. Where's the hot food?" And then, how everyone (but not the cat) would laugh. How long ago those days are now!

A couple of weeks later, Bush won the 2004 election, the Democrats having nominated another drab defeatist, John Kerry. It had been a close election like that of 2000. It was to that Buckeye State, Ohio, that Bush owned his final victory. Democrats, of course, and as usual, alleged voter fraud. The next day driving down the highway a local business had erected a large sign to be seen by all travelers: "BOYCOTT OHIO." "Here we go again," I thought to myself -- that some of these people must never have played high school sports, that they never got a bloody nose in a football game or broke their arm in basketball practice. They have never fought for a rebound or crashed into the catcher at home plate trying to score. They have never encouraged a teammate who just messed up a play. They have never been yelled at by a totally pissed-off coach. They have never gone through a baseball season where they won only 3 games out of 21. They have never been cut by a coach because they were too small or missed too many practices. But, more than anything else, it is clear that they do not know how to lose, these new Vermonters who have never played sports and have descended upon Vermont, because anyone who has played sports knows that sometimes you win and sometimes you lose.

CONCLUSION

A number of funny stories have been omitted, which is not very smart, so here goes!

There is that whole notion of the Second Republic: yes, a movement exists in Vermont saying that it ought to secede from the Union, mirroring its colonial day status as an independent republic. This laughable idea is taken seriously by thousands of Vermonters and it receives constant rejuvenation from crazy websites and irrational letters to the editor. Maybe we <u>should</u> let them go!

We have not spoken enough about drugs. Vermont is a drug friendly culture. Not only does it serve as a pharmaceutical conduit between New York and Montreal, but, generally speaking, for consumption within the state, anti-drug lows are commonly ignored. The state Attorney General has better things to do, so he looks, too often, the other way. The police and prosecutors are lax. Once again, this lazy attitude can be traced back to the dialectic: impulse restraint vs. impulse release. In other words, "go ahead and enjoy yourself." Hedonism is the governing principal. As long as you are not a major distributor, the law leaves you alone. Liberal judges and prosecutors do not want to have the court system clogged with relatively minor drug offences, so they choose not to prosecute. But, I say: if the law is not to be enforced, rescind it.

One day I was spraying my fruit trees to prevent fungus, mold and scabs. As an experienced California fruit grower of oranges, grapes and pistachios, it is something I do every two weeks in the Spring and early Summer. As I was spraying, a neighbor approached and said that she wished I would not do that, because the spray drifts and diffuses over her garden, and that the spray was not good for her body. I said that I was not interesting in growing diseased fruit, but that I would try to spray on windless days. I told her as well that I would never tell her what to do on her land. Her expression registered anger: I had defied her eco-tenets.

Transgenderism is another issue that is coming to the fore. Increasingly, young people, convinced by some strange cult that they posses the wrong skin, are going under the knife and taking handfuls of hormones to change their sex. Immediately, these same defaced young people demand their rights, in housing and employment, to not be look at askance. Does not a landlord or employer have the right to not rent or to not have someone who has chosen this path? But more importantly, why can't the young people resist these cult-driven desires to so deface themselves? Can they not tame these urges, or are these urges to rule them with society to accede? Once again desire and impulse release are paramount; self-control and impulse restraint are forgotten.

Another thing: Vermont is not the Green Mountain State; it is the Grant State, as in: "If you move to Vermont, they will give you a grant for planting your flowerbed or blowing your nose!" One would have to live in the capital, Montpelier, or monitor the computer <u>daily</u> to see what new grant giveaway program, no matter how esoteric the cause, that the social engineers masquerading as legislators, have just dreamed up. No matter how foolish the project, funds will be found and thus, a state of sissies, those who do not earn an income through hard work, is thus brought forth.

Why can't the cheese mongers, instead of approaching the legislators (re: social engineers) asking them for money like unemployed and lazy teenagers, from their own cheese cooperatives with their own money? Because, going to the state and asking for a handout is easier. Because, they feel entitled. Because, they know, often living in the Grant State for decades, a place where the Victim Mentality is everywhere, that if you ask for some money, it shall be given to you. (Apologies to the Bible.) The cheese people forget that once they take the state's money, the state will soon be telling them how to farm, how to make cheese, what kind of tractor to use and how much diesel they can use. That loss of freedom is discounted as they join the gravy train which never stops rolling through the station.

I used to joke with people that Governor Jim Douglas, whom I know slightly and who is a very decent fellow trying hard to stop foolish spending and to stem some of these deranged trends, called me up on the telephone and suggested in a low conspiratorial tone: "Dominic, I know that you are not happy here. Perhaps it would be better for all of us if you were to leave." (A little like in <u>Godfather II</u> when the consigliere tells Franco Pentangeli that it would be a good idea to take a hot bath and slit his wrists!) Douglas never made the call, but whenever I tell the joke, this <u>fiction</u>, the listener thinks it to be true!

My parents have, up till now, been under represented: clearly, they have formed my thoughts. Over countless dinner tables they encouraged the free flow of debate. They probed, cajoled and teased us children. Never mocking or grandstanding, they drew forth our fledgling incipient ideas, if you want to call them that. Not one of us were ever made fun of or demeaned. My father, especially, would point out frail logic, faulty reasoning, or the foolish disclaimer. My mother, in particular, would note the instance of poor grammar or weak diction. Both encouraged, always, the back-and-forth of debate and denounced one of us if we mocked another. Over those many years now long ago, we discussed all sorts of things; capitalism vs. communism, immigration policy, how large the safety net ought to be and what does it mean for a nation to be ready militarily. This was when I was five! They drew forth our own opinions and gently poked them if they were foolish. Most importantly they instructed us, by deed and example, that all people are entitled to speak their minds, that all of us have a unique voice which ought to be heard and never ignored. They told us that you can disagree with someone, once you have patiently heard his viewpoint but that that disagreement should never harm the friendship. They, finally, made the most important point: never mock another's view.

So it is with this sort of mind-set, one favoring free speech and friendly debate, that we arrived in Vermont. You have read what we witnessed: the hostility, the mocking insularity, the intransigence. But, here I must stress again the sharp demarcation that exists between the old and new Vermonters. The old ones are fine - akin to frugal, hard-working people across our country. They want government small and not to be told what to do or how to think. How sad they must be to have lost their state! The new Vermonters now lead the state in every important category.

And I guess that leads to another and final point: you are only in these people's good books if you agree with them right down the line, on every issue. If you deviate from their progressive canon in the smallest instance, they will tell you about it. May I call them NDL's: non-debating liberals? Rather than participate in the ebb-and-flow of normal conversation when disagreements always take place (and are quickly forgotten), the new Vermonter retreats to extreme websites for bolstering, confirmation, affirmation. There, for hours at a time, they can re-learn the canon, study all the new rules, because for them, these extreme political perspectives have become their new religion, which is impossible since there is no mention of a deity.

I noticed that three years after the 2000 election, Gore bumper stickers were still everywhere. Similarly, three years after the 2004 election Kerry stickers were equally popular. What does this say? Many of these people are poor losers.

Maybe they did not play many high school basketball games where they got their clock cleaned, like I did! When Al Gore was slow to concede the 2000 election, he set a tone: it is good to be a poor loser and this lamentable cancer engendered by Gore's foot-dragging has contaminated our nation: He should be ashamed to so play the victim. Be a man and admit you lost. Nixon might have contested the equally tight 1960 election but he knew to do so would necessarily harm the nation. Again, (Read Horowitz) Gore was not so magnanimous; sadly, his selfish example became the example or standard for his followers: this is how you behave; this is how you act: play the victim. "You do not have to respect a sitting president." So, many new Vermonters surely do not. It is a kick, were it not upsetting, to drive around Vermont and study the backs of cars: many have 10 or 15 or 20 bumper stickers preaching extreme points of view, pushing some arcane cause or calling the president a liar. One can only concede some of the drivers must be infused with what can only be called hate.

All of which brings me to my final and obvious point: if we are to be a new nation, new ways of speaking with one another must be arrived at. The all-or-nothing credo must be eliminated, now! The tone of discussion should begin to include mirth and self-deprecation (Can you imagine it?) Animosity must be replaced with curiosity. The overall tone must be made more civil. Judgment must be restrained since, as S.I. Hayakawa says, "It stops thought." Probing questions must return and blanket generalities must depart. Can there be a return to a thoughtful and lively intelligence where we respect, not demean, the other's views? Vermont ought to be a free and open state where people who disagree politely, yet strenuously, can live side-by-side in tolerance and mutual respect. This eagerness to condemn must be curtailed and the willingness to deride controlled. Nuance and complexities of judgement must return. Ought Vermont to be a bastion only for those new Vermonters who believe that the counter culture with all of its progressive tenets is an ersatz religion? When will the rights of old Vermonters to express themselves again be respected? Ought Vermont to be the kind of place where ideas are exchanged and the other person's point of view is actually considered? Obviously I believe that the latter is the correct course, but for that to happen, a much greater tolerance must be engendered and put to use. That virtue now is sadly in short supply. From where shall it spring, from what dark unused recess of the human heart shall it flow? As my parents told me: "Isn't everyone permitted to have and express his own opinion?" Who will take the first step or start the first trickle?

CODA

Not intentionally, I have not said much about my mother. Why does she pertain to this discussion?

Like many, she was the kind of mom always in the background, preparing meals and giving all her children (then, there were four of us), the extra portion, the ripest orange, the toast with the most slathered butter. She was smiling and gracious on every occasion and she only scolded us, raising her voice but a little, when what we had done had truly warranted it. Kind, well above normalcy, she never seemed to think about herself or her own happiness. At the many large and extravagant parties that my parents threw during those now-distant years, she always sought out the shy person standing alone and she would make friendly conversation with that person, trying to put him or her at ease. Throughout her abbreviated life she took tremendous care of her children, us, as well as our feisty and difficult dad and thought little of herself.

So, one must ask: What was the source of her boundless altruism? From what incident or philosophy stems her refusal to be egocentric? Why was she the distinct opposite of some who say, with no apparent tongue-in-cheek, "If I am happy, the world is happy."

To understand, one must, of course, retreat to the past. When she was in nursing school in the 1930s, either in North Dakota or Minnesota (Is that, in itself, not sad? – that I do not know in which state she took her courses. How quickly the sands of time cover the lazy Phoenix.), my mom contracted tuberculosis, a condition at that time, unbeknownst to her and the other nursing students around her. She, whose name was Florence, used to tell me later that it had been close contact in burn wards with Indians: the Dakotas, the Mandans and the Sioux, that had done it. How did they get there?, I now wonder. Presumably, or so I now conjure, the Indians must have consumed too much alcohol, and they had been smoking or perhaps around a campfire, and stupid fights had broken out, leading to unguarded flames and, finally, inadvertent self-immolation. At the wards, bending down to administer gauze and ointments and cream, supplicatory help and care, the TB bacteria had gone from the lungs and mouth of the Indians to the lungs and mouth of my mother, an unseen trek. Both had been bent down low, close to the ground, as if lost in a begging prayer. Infection is a quiet, unnoticed voyage of bacteria or virus from one host to another. Yet, she did not know any of this at the time. She looked hale, it was mid-Depression and she had just met my father. While dating, neither knew that she was very sick.

Ten years passed. It was 1943. They had married, and quickly, two children were born. The first was to die of leukemia, age 5, and the second was born severely handicapped by Down's Syndrome. My father was in the Navy then, working as a navigator in the South Pacific, and he would have found out about the death and the unprovidential birth only after many months had passed. Therefore, Florence would have had to carry these pervasive deep burdens largely alone. How lonely she must have felt as the war dragged on! Happily, a third child arrived that year and this one was healthy. He was my brother, Tom.

Then, in 1945, after the Germans surrendered and as President Truman was deciding whether to bomb Japan with "this new, strange device," and with my father still at sea, probably off the coast of Tasmania or Zanzibar, my mom ran into my Uncle Bill, my dad's younger brother; he was a brilliant doctor, an inventive wit and impatient political scientist.

This is a saucy story of the family, only perhaps true, that they, before my father arrived on the scene, used to date. Do I know this, without a doubt, to be unembellished? How much is fabricated, manufactured from cloudy mist? Doubts persist, yet it is too rich a tale not to be told. So, then, when he says to her, "Florence, take off your shirt!" She, naturally, feeling the faithful constraints of the matrimonial bond said, "Bill, no! I am married to your brother! I can't do that!" Bill was, as always, alert, determined, focused. Without a glimmer of a smile, or the suggestion of a lewd wink, he said, "Florence, take off your shirt. This is a medical question, please. Now!"

And, so it was on that summer's day in 1945, close to the bombings of Nagasaki and Hiroshima (which would lead within a week to Japan's surrender), so it was that my mom was diagnosed with disease: my Uncle Bill told her then that she had an advanced case of tuberculosis. At that instant, my mom gave away any idea of a healthy life. From that instant forward, all was changed unalterably. Soon, she entered a series of Navy sanitoria up and down the West Coast, from Seattle to San Diego. Mostly, the nurses put her "on ice": treatment was poor and the anti-TB drugs were still experimental. The various treatments would stun the bacteria, and yet, soon, they would creep back, mustering, assembling in battalions, or, as Albert Camus writes in The Plague,

> "That the plague bacillus never dies or disappears
> for good; that it can lie dormant for years and years
> in furniture and linen chests; that it bides its time in
> bedrooms, cellars, trunks and bookshelves; and that
> perhaps the day would come when for the bane and
> the enlightening of men, it would rouse up its rats
> again and send them forth to die in a happy city." (P.
> 278 *Modern Library*, 1948)

But how can one talk about the "enlightening of man," when my mom was so sick?

After that, mostly, she lingered, unhealed and unhealing, sleeping in scores of strange beds, attended to only by strangers, (Did the muses smile or were they grim?) lost in the strong unyielding grip of this pernicious disease, one most chronic and energy-sapping. At the same time, my father stayed at home tending to my older brother, Tom. He fought his own grey and lurking demons, those unappealing ghosts, trying to advance financially and avoid that other creeping Irish monster of too much drink. Ah, to forget and not remember all the sour times of the past! Is that not a sign of health?

Finally, in 1950, her pulmonary doctor advised my parents that my mother would need surgery, immediately. Progress to stem the course of the disease had not occurred. A pneumonectomy was performed, removing one and a third of her lungs. My mother was left with only two-thirds of one lung; all the other tissue had become necrotic. Two-thirds of a lung would support my mother for her remaining thirty one years; henceforth, she was always short of breath. She would never again be the athlete she once had been. She would never again posses a virgin scarless body: inch-wide, medium blue scars, the color of the Caspian or cerulean, cris-crossed her chest. She would never again have the smart feline curves she once had had. Indeed, from that point in time's march onward, she would wear a blanket pad on her back, adding an inch or so of form to her figure. As a boy, watching her dress, I can remember her putting on this small pad. In their small bedroom I can remember the many wide blue scars of her chest. I can remember, too, that she always wore a smile. But, how marred she was! How disfigured! Yet, she did not think so. She would have, then, expelled that useless thought from her mind. She would never have used those words to describe her condition. She simply felt, like Roy Campanella, the Brooklyn Dodgers catcher from the 1950's who was paralyzed in a car accident, that "It's Good to be Alive!" (Roy Campanella. It's Good to be Alive. Boston: Little Brown and Company, 1959)

The point of this reminiscence is to answer these questions: why or how or what? Why did my mother not grovel in despair? How was she able to resist assigning blame to the Indians, for she never said a word against them? What gave to her that kindness and strength?

After the surgery and her quick recovery, my parents surged once more into each others' arms and produced three more children, myself and my two younger sisters. We, and our older brother, Tom all gathered as a beacon, became her light. We were her light as she became a stoic, that is, someone who does not complain, a person indifferent to grief or pain. She was content in this world and only saw joy through our eyes. Unlike so many people of today, she did not demand to be happy. Always, she thought more of her children than herself. She always gave to me the larger portion of scrambled eggs or the bigger glass of milk. Years passed: we children grew up and left the house free to make our own mistakes and small successes. It was a shame when she died, aged only sixty-seven, in November of 1981, her body shrunken from a lack of oxygen; that death meant we as a family would no longer have her direction and durable spirit to guide us and we all would pay a heavy price for that lacuna.

By contrast, children: my generation, we have largely escheured them. They are a pain in the rear, too expensive, distracting. They will take me from my interests! Vermonters, especially, have avoided them, giving that state one of the lowest birth rates in the country.

To not have children means that these baby-boomers are free (if I may use that word: re: Satre and Auberon Waugh, "I am condemned to be free") to concentrate only on themselves, to pursue whatever strange course that temporarily appeals, perhaps jumping from one rutted or mean intoxication to the next, a decision, unmet, which can only be an unseen trap or mere mischief. Who will lead? How to decide? Solipsism: the theory that the self is the only thing that can be known or verified. Pleasure: what new form lurks? And what if it doth fade?

Avoiding children, choosing various false divinities, they think, as all practicing egocentrics do, that if I am happy, then the world is happy, not knowing that serving others gives a more lasting satisfaction.

Too, so determined is their concentration on themselves, they have planned to eliminate God from their lives. His gracious rules they see as constraints to an unfettered life. Obedience: the word is no longer uttered! They say, "Should I not be free to follow my own chosen course to happiness?" And thus, the path to solipsism is laid out and people in Vermont and elsewhere, thereby jump from one rut to another, looking for happiness, I presume, avoiding God, and children equally. What if that path curves? What if the road is reverse cambered?

Stoicism in the face of desire or the death of a child is replaced by self-absorption and, when that does not work, complaining and whining. How Vermonters complain and whine, some of them, that is, and not the old stoics, those at once taciturn and restrained from days gone by.

So, all manner of replacement religions sprout. Let us make a list:

[NOT COMPLETE!]

1. All rock music
2. Meditation
3. All machiato and other coffee drinks (How do you grind your beans?)
4. Whole grains including quinoa, frik, and teff
5. Business and the pursuit of money
6. Flat stomachs
7. I Ching
8. Martial Arts
9. Paiute Indian funeral practices
10. The occult and massage
11. Sexual deviation of every measure
12. Vegetarianism
13. Daily drugs of choice
14. Marilyn Monroe
15. Hymns, holms and hadj
16. Various dance steps including the Urkel and the Hucklebuck
17. Extreme environmentalism and anything called organic

    And last, but not least,

18. Political progressivism

Yet, how could one expert to derive spiritual sustenance from these things? Of course, these are not religions, but they are, nonetheless, thought to be so by far too many.

Those in Vermont who have embraced these ersatz religions might be wise to rethink that choice. Instead of abandoning God, why not bring Him back? Consider that his rules may make life a bit easier.

Too, we must all engender a stoicism as my mother did. It served her well. Do not always ask, "Am I happy?" Who cares? Remember the Stephen Crone short story, "The Open Boot." Its theme states that <u>the</u> world <u>is</u> <u>indifferent</u> <u>to</u> <u>our</u> <u>fate</u>. The world does not care what we wish for. Such arrogance exists: how is it that we think that we may bend the world to conform to our meager will? Is that not a supreme sin of pride? To counter that, one must recall Socrates' statement that the only important question in life is to what extent one ought to be humble.

To garner and collect the strength necessary to live in this world, we must be strong and stoical in the face of Sisyphean difficulties and challenges, and not give in to depression and anxiety. But how is one to engender strength? From whence shall it flow? Assuredly, it cannot come from me since I am weak and my thoughts are but paltry. On John F. Kennedy's desk rested a coconut, taken from the island in the South Pacific when he and his crew had been stranded for days; it's carved with the inscription, "Oh, God. The sea is so great and my boat is so small."

What, then, must we do?: Bring children into the world. They will be the mischievious errant ones to lead us away from our selfishness, they will take us away from silly ruts, of coffee or roux and they will show to us in their keen and eager faces God's light. That light will guide our way and, especially while they are small and before the problematic teenage years, who cannot delight in the smile of a child? What parent does not wish to safeguard that innocence? Who does not wish to see a child grow up strong and resourceful? Again, who cannot feel the same affection for a child as James Joyce felt one hundred years ago for his son, Giorgio, while watching him bathe and frolic "On the Baths of Fontana" in Trieste:

> "From whining wind and colder
> Grey sea I wrap him warm
> And touch his trembling fineboned shoulder
> And boyish arm.
>
> Around us fear, descending
> Darkness of fear above
> And in my heart how deep unending
> Ache of love."

Trieste 1914

What parent cannot feel that overwhelming instinct to protect? Thus, we are taken out of ourselves, that this self-absorption of today might dissipate, and that will be a good thing for all of our culture.

Finally, what more needs to be said to end this winter's tale or curt admonition? Plainly, that we need suffering to learn anything, just as a runner needs painful training to be swift. If we shall lack suffering, everyday we shall become more lax and dull.

Our generation, unlike our parents, has had an easy life with no Depression, only distant wars fought by others, infrequent illness. Therefore, automatically, we have become predictably weak. But, is it not better to be strong? Indeed, should we not, paradoxically, ask for challenges so that we may become always more stout?

My mother did not ask for the disease which marked her life, yet it came nonetheless, to her. No doubt chagrined, still, she never shrank from it, she never complained and she never asked God to have it lifted from her. This illness of hers led her to ask God for help, always, and it gave to her a stronger faith: God became her companion as she battled. In the end, because of her illness and, then, her growing faith, she was a person stronger, better and kinder. She used to say (along with Roberto Clemente's mother, by the way), "Only God makes me happy. Life is nothing. Everything ends. God makes men happy." (Read David Maranis's <u>Clemente</u>: <u>The</u> <u>Passive</u> <u>and</u> <u>Grace</u> <u>of</u> <u>Baseball's</u> <u>Last</u> <u>Hero</u>. New York: Simon & Schuster, 2006) Like Kennedy, she realized she was a tiny open boat on a very large sea. Is it not time for us to think so?

Why do we think that life is meant to be easy? Because we have become soft, we do not expect it to be hard. If we toughen ourselves and expect less, then, when difficulties arise, say, an illness, or the death of a child or a financial crisis, then, when those things happen, and if God is at my side, then and only then we will be ready enough to say, "Let us join the battle!"

Or, as Winston Churchill says, let us have "no more fear. KBO. Keep Buggering On!"